MYSTERIES
of HISTORY

An Inca mask.

MYSTERIES
of HISTORY

Historian Robert Stewart Ph.D.
with Clint Twist and Edward Horton

NATIONAL GEOGRAPHIC

WASHINGTON, D.C.

A Marshall Edition
Conceived, edited, and designed by Marshall Editions
The Old Brewery, 6 Blundell Street, London N7 9BH, U.K.
www.quarto.com

First published in North America in 2003 by
The National Geographic Society
1145 17th Street N.W.
Washington, D.C. 20036

ISBN 0-7922-6232-8

Library of Congress Cataloging-in-Publication Data available on request.

Originated in Singapore by Chromagraphics
Printed and bound in China by Midas Printing Limited

Design: Karen Bowen
Maps: Carl Mehler, Director of Maps, National Geographic Books;
Joseph F. Ochlak, Map Researcher and Editor; Matt Chwastyk, Map Production
Picture research: ISI (Image Select International Ltd)
Commissioning editor: Jeremy Harwood
Copy-editing: Michael Axworthy
Americanization: Constance Novis
Indexing: Hilary Bird

One of the world's largest nonprofit scientific and educational organizations, the National Geographic
Society was founded in 1888 "for the increase and diffusion of geographic knowledge."
Fulfilling this mission, the Society educates and inspires millions every day through its magazines,
books, television programs, videos, maps and atlases, research grants, the National Geographic Bee,
teacher workshops, and innovative classroom materials. The Society is supported through membership
dues, charitable gifts, and income from the sale of its educational products. This support is vital
to National Geographic's mission to increase global understanding and promote conservation of our
planet through exploration, research, and education.

For more information, please call 1-800-NGS LINE (647-5463) or write to the following address:

National Geographic Society
1145 17th Street N.W.
Washington, D.C. 20036-4688 U.S.A.

Visit the Society's Web site at www.nationalgeographic.com.

Did Custer and the Sioux chief Crazy Horse
actually fight hand to hand at the Battle of the
Little Bighorn? See pp. 148–157.

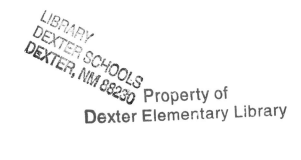

CONTENTS

Did the Greeks really build the legendary Trojan horse? See pp. 34–41.

MAPS

Everyone knows the legend of King Arthur and his knights of the Round Table. But is it just a story or did he really exist? See pp. 52–59.

CONTRIBUTORS

AUTHORS

Robert Stewart, Ph.D., is a graduate of Toronto University, in Ontario, Canada, and of Oxford University, in England, where he studied modern history and modern languages. He has been assistant professor of history at Canada's University of Saskatchewan and a research lecturer at the University of London's Westfield College. He was elected an Honorary Fellow of St. Anthony's College, Oxford University, in 1973. His publications include the *Europa Dictionary of Political Quotations*, *Party and Politics*, and *Ideas that Shaped Our World*.

Edward Horton was born and educated in Canada, where he studied history and politics at Queen's University, in Kingston, Ontario. He has spent the past 30 years as an editor and editorial director at various British publishing houses, including Orbis and Marshall Cavendish. He is the author of a dozen books on subjects ranging from history to sports.

Clint Twist studied history at Cambridge University and worked as a journalist, museum consultant, and historian before becoming a full-time author in 1988. He has written more than 40 books. Most recently he authored *Atlas of the Celts* and co-authored *Civilizations*, which covers 10,000 years of human history.

CONSULTANTS

Dr. James Annesley is senior lecturer at the School of Humanities at Kingston University, in Surrey, England, and associate lecturer at the Institute of United States Studies at the University of London. He specializes in 19th- and 20th-century American culture and is the author of *Blank Fictions: Culture, Consumption and Contemporary America* as well as articles in a number of journals.

Dr. Paul G. Bahn studied archaeology at Cambridge University, in England, and earned post-doctoral fellowships at Liverpool and London Universities as well as a J. Paul Getty Fellowship in the history of art and the humanities. He is now a full-time writer, editor, and translator. His books include *Ancient Places* (with Professor Glyn Daniel), *Images of the Ice Age*, *Journey Through Time* (both with Jean Vertut), *Archaeology: Theories, Methods and Practice* (with Professor Colin Renfrew), and the *Cambridge Illustrated History of Prehistoric Art*.

Dr. Andrea Hopkins studied English at Oxford University, in England, where she wrote a thesis on penitence in medieval romance. Her many books include *Knights* and *The Chronicles of King Arthur*. She has contributed to encyclopedias of the Middle Ages and the Renaissance and is presently writing a historical novel about Eleanor of Aquitaine. She lives in Oxford with her daughter.

Dr. Lars Peter Laamann is an ESRC research fellow and a lecturer in the history department of the School of Oriental and African Studies at the University of London. His research areas are 17th- to 19th-century Chinese history, society, and religion.

Dr. Richard Sims has taught Japanese history at the School of Oriental and African Studies at the University of London since 1966. He was awarded a Ph.D. in 1968 and has published four books on modern Japanese history.

INTRODUCTION

The writing of history is difficult for many reasons. Chief among them is that there are no "right" answers. The past is often reluctant to offer up its secrets. It may be a relatively simple matter to establish a basic chronology of events— when battles were won or lost, the rise and fall of governments, the making of laws—but beyond that bare skeleton of the historical record, arguments about interpretation among historians, gaps in our knowledge, and baffling questions that seem to elude explanation are all commonplace.

So history has many mysteries. They arise for a variety of reasons. Sometimes the evidence is so patchy that different historians are left having to piece together the jigsaw with many of the most important pieces missing. Naturally, the pictures they come up with can vary widely. There will never be one, true account of the decline and fall of the Roman Empire. And the debate about whether Marco Polo ever actually got to China will continue to rage. Sometimes the evidence has been deliberately destroyed or distorted by participants in events in order to prevent the truth emerging. Thanks to the decision of Chinese officials completely to destroy the records of their seafarers' exploits in the first three decades of the 15th century, whether the Chinese beat Columbus to America remains a mystery, the answer dependent on what might be called secondhand evidence. In our own time, the most flagrant attempt to muddy the historical waters was conducted by the Warren Commission, the C.I.A., and the F.B.I. We may never solve the mystery of

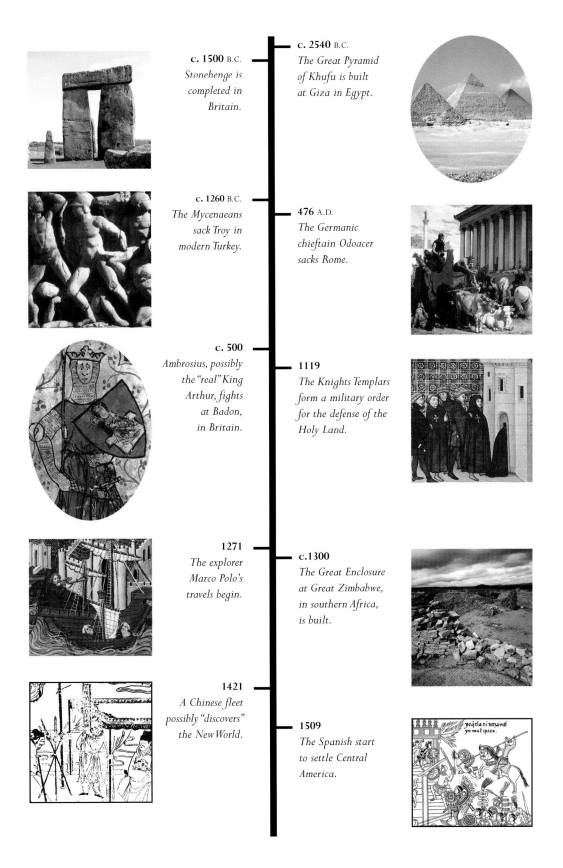

c. 2540 B.C.
*The Great Pyramid
of Khufu is built
at Giza in Egypt.*

c. 1500 B.C.
*Stonehenge is
completed in
Britain.*

c. 1260 B.C.
*The Mycenaeans
sack Troy in
modern Turkey.*

476 A.D.
*The Germanic
chieftain Odoacer
sacks Rome.*

c. 500
*Ambrosius, possibly
the "real" King
Arthur, fights
at Badon,
in Britain.*

1119
*The Knights Templars
form a military order
for the defense of the
Holy Land.*

1271
*The explorer
Marco Polo's
travels begin.*

c.1300
*The Great Enclosure
at Great Zimbabwe,
in southern Africa,
is built.*

1421
*A Chinese fleet
possibly "discovers"
the New World.*

1509
*The Spanish start
to settle Central
America.*

who killed John F. Kennedy, though it will not be from want of trying.

There is, too, a broader consideration. Facts are like sacks, wrote the English historian E.H. Carr. They don't stand up until you put something in them. Different cultures, different eras, different individuals, bring their own different intellectual contexts to the study of the past. So distinguished a medieval chronicler as Geoffrey of Monmouth speculated that Stonehenge, in Wiltshire, England, was probably the work of an extinct race of giants. Today some theorists argue that it was constructed with extraterrestrial assistance. The answers that historians find depend upon the questions that they ask. It simply never occurred to most 19th-century white explorers in southern Africa to consider that so impressive a city as Great Zimbabwe could have been built by African "savages." Nor, though the evidence from Native Americans was there, was it easy for white Americans—or profitable for Hollywood's film studios—to believe that Custer's "last stand" was anything less than heroic.

Those last two mysteries have now been solved, but other questions will continue to hang in the air. What lies behind the building of the pyramids? How much truth is mixed with legend in the tales of King Arthur and his court? Whatever the answers, the investigation of controversial episodes that have puzzled historians down the years makes fascinating reading for anyone interested in the shadowy events of the past.

By Robert Stewart, Ph.D., 2003

1585
Sir Richard Grenville leads an expedition to Roanoke in North America.

1612
In Japan, the shogun Ieyasu issues an edict against Christianity.

1788
In England, George III suffers his first outbreak of "madness."

1821
The French ex-emperor Napoleon dies on St. Helena in the Atlantic.

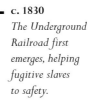

c. 1830
The Underground Railroad first emerges, helping fugitive slaves to safety.

1876
The Battle of the Little Bighorn takes place in the U.S.A.

1937
The Hindenburg *airship crashes, killing 36.*

1941
The Japanese attack on Pearl Harbor brings the U.S.A. into World War II.

1963
President John F. Kennedy is assassinated in Dallas, Texas.

WHY DID THE PHARAOHS BUILD THE PYRAMIDS?

Egypt's great pyramids are unique. No other ancient wonders have been the subject of so much controversy. Who built them and how? What was their purpose? Were they even the work of the ancient Egyptians at all? What happened to the rich treasures they must once have contained? Over the years, the pyramids have surrendered some of their secrets, but there are still some unsolved mysteries.

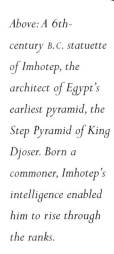

Above: A 6th-century B.C. statuette of Imhotep, the architect of Egypt's earliest pyramid, the Step Pyramid of King Djoser. Born a commoner, Imhotep's intelligence enabled him to rise through the ranks.

The story starts in around 2630 B.C., when Djoser, the ruling pharaoh of the time, ordered the construction of a new kind of burial place. It was to be grander than the underground tombs or the low, flat mudbrick buildings called mastabas, in which most previous rulers of Egypt had been buried. Djoser had been successful in war, and his expanding kingdom was prosperous enough to afford what he had in mind. But there was more to the story than a simple desire for self-aggrandizement. It was also Djoser's way of making sure that, as a living god, he was properly equipped for the afterlife. For the ancient Egyptians, death was simply the beginning of a journey to another world, and it was vital that their rulers in particular set off on it as well prepared as possible.

Djoser's chief minister, Imhotep, was the man put in charge of the task. He turned out to be an inspired architect, and the world's first pyramid was the result of his labors. It started off as a normal mastaba-type structure, but, as work progressed, it was enlarged by adding one mastaba on top of another until it consisted of six individual "steps" in all, reaching a height of some 200 feet (60 meters). Hence the name by which it is known to history—the Step Pyramid. The superstructure was made of small limestone blocks and desert clay. Inside, the burial chamber and storage spaces for Djoser's grave

Opposite: The pyramids at Giza. Why the Egyptians stopped building pyramids on such a scale is not certain, but it may have been due to declining prosperity. Below: A statue of King Djoser from the mastaba near his Step Pyramid.

"*Think of it, soldiers! From the summit of these pyramids, forty centuries of history are looking down upon us!*"

NAPOLEON BONAPARTE BEFORE THE BATTLE OF THE PYRAMIDS, 1798

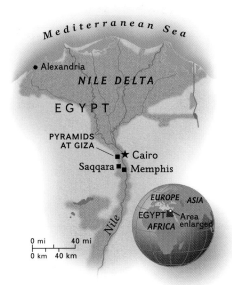

goods were carved out of the earth and rock. The intention was to copy the structure of Djoser's own palace. The central area was the burial place. The surrounding rooms contained burial artifacts, such as furniture, jewelry, and other favorite treasures owned by the king.

Just how Imhotep decided on his plan will probably never be known. Maybe he simply seized the chance to make use of the resources of manpower, new materials, and tools that were at his disposal, but some experts believe that there may have been a deeper, more spiritual intent behind his grand design. According to them, the Step Pyramid was a ladder—not a symbol of a ladder but an actual one—by which a dead ruler's soul could climb into the sky to join the gods in immortality. It was literally a stairway to heaven.

A few years later, around 2540 B.C., the next important development took place, when the pharaoh Khufu commissioned the building of the largest pyramid of all. This became known to history as the Great Pyramid. Some 754 feet (230 meters) square and 479 feet (146 meters) high, it is the last surviving wonder of the Seven Wonders of the Ancient World.

Like his predecessors, Khufu began work on planning his "house of eternity" as soon as he came to the throne. The first decision he made was where to build it. His choice fell on Giza on the west bank of the Nile, just a few miles north of the Step Pyramid at Saqqara. Burial places were usually built on the west bank because the sun "died" on the western horizon every night. Giza was also conveniently located close to quarries from which some, though not all, of the 2,300,000 blocks of stone that would be needed to build the pyramid could be obtained.

The pyramid is believed to have taken about 30 years to build and involved a massive workforce. The Greek historian Herodotus, who visited Egypt in around 450 B.C., claimed that as many as 100,000 captive slaves labored on the site. Present-

Below: The Step Pyramid of King Djoser at Saqqara was the world's first pyramid. Its design was altered during construction as its builders got used to working with stone rather than the traditional mudbricks they were used to. The result was six giant steps rising high above the desert. Experts believe they symbolize creation, or a stairway to heaven.

Opposite (top): The ruins of the Step Pyramid funerary complex. No pyramid complex was complete without its ceremonial buildings, linked by long walkways. Some of the most important buildings at the Step Pyramid were copies of sacred shrines that stood elsewhere in Upper and Lower Egypt. Opposite (below): The golden lid of Tutankhamun's inner coffin shows what riches the Egyptian pharaohs took with them to their graves.

Egypt		The World
	c.11,000 B.C.	*The earliest known pottery is made in Japan.*
	c.9000 B.C.	*The first farmers appear in Mesopotamia (now Iraq).*
	c.7000 B.C.	*Çatal Hüyük, possibly the world's first town, emerges in Anatolia.*
	c.4500 B.C.	*The first megalithic tombs are constructed in western Europe.*
	c.3400 B.C.	*The earliest forms of writing develop in Mesopotamia.*
Egypt's first walled towns are built. c.3300 B.C.		
The earliest hieroglyphic script is used in Egypt. c.3200 B.C.		
Egypt is unified by King Narmer, who becomes the first pharaoh. c.3100 B.C.	c.3000 B.C.	*The potter's wheel is invented in China.*
The world's first pyramid, the Step Pyramid of King Djoser, is built by the architect Imhotep. c.2630 B.C.	c.2600 B.C.	*Temple complexes are built along the Andean coast in South America.*
The Great Pyramid of Khufu is built at Giza. c.2540 B.C.		
The Sphinx, the earliest monumental sculpture, is carved. c.2500 B.C.	c.2300 B.C.	*The world's first empire is established among the city states of Mesopotamia, under the leadership of Sargon of Agade.*
	c.1750 B.C.	*The Babylonian ruler Hammurabi publishes his Code of Laws, the first in the world.*
The Egyptian rulers and their nobles are buried in rock-hewn tombs in the Valley of the Kings near Luxor. c.1570 B.C.	c.1500 B.C.	*Stonehenge is completed in England.*
The Jewish exodus from Egypt ends in Palestine. c.1200 B.C.	c.1200 B.C.	*Mesoamerica's first great civilization, the Olmecs, emerges in what is now Mexico.*
Ramses III, the last great pharaoh, dies. 1166 B.C.		
Civil war leads to Egypt's dissolution into small states. 945 B.C.		

"There are writings in the pyramid indicating how much was spent on radishes and onions and garlic for the workmen, and I am sure that the interpreter said 1,600 talents of silver had been paid."

GREEK HISTORIAN HERODOTUS ON THE REWARDS GIVEN TO THE WORKMEN ON THE GREAT PYRAMID, 5TH CENTURY B.C.

day Egyptologists believe the number of workers was more like 30,000 and, contrary to popular belief, they were not slaves. Some of the men became part of the permanent workforce, but others were called on only when the Nile was in flood. At that time, farming all but ceased and the transportation of stone blocks was easiest. Some workers were assigned to the granite quarries in the far south; others to the limestone quarries across the Nile from Giza. Some remained laborers, others were trained as masons, while a few were found to be good managers and became officials. There was a permanent workforce of around 15,000 housed in a small town nearby, and up to 15,000 seasonal workers were available at any one time. Many of the former spent their entire working lives on the project—and they were proud to take part in it. Nor were their labors limited to the Great Pyramid itself.

For the ancient Egyptians, a pyramid was the main part of a complex religious machine, intended to give a dead pharaoh the best possible "launch" to the heavens, its shape possibly symbolizing the slanting rays of the sun. So each pyramid was the symbolic centerpiece for a surrounding complex of ceremonial halls, temples, and linking processional courtyards and causeways that were not just used for the burial ritual, but also for festivals that celebrated the pharaoh's accession long after his death. In this way each pharaoh added to the spiritual glue that held Egypt together. The Great Pyramid was also the hub of a number of special cemeteries specifically intended for members of the royal court and the top officials of state.

The amount of building involved was staggering. So, too, was the accuracy with which it was accomplished. With its sides facing directly north, south, east, and west, the Great Pyramid is so mathematically exact in its construction that all kinds of weird and wonderful speculations have arisen as a result. In the mid-19th century, for instance, a British astronomer named Charles Piazzi Smyth claimed that the ancient Egyptians had encoded numerous prophesies into the dimensions of the Great Pyramid and that he had decoded them. Some have suggested that, rather than as a tomb, the pyramid was built as a

Above: This Solar Boat was discovered buried in a pit close to the Great Pyramid in 1982. It was in bits when it was found, but has since been reconstructed. Experts think the ancient Egyptians put it there for Khufu to use to travel to the afterlife. Opposite: The Great Pyramid at Giza (center) was home of Khufu's huge red granite sarcophagus. Over the centuries, the pyramid lost its outer covering of limestone. Much of it was stripped away and used for various building programs in the city of Cairo.

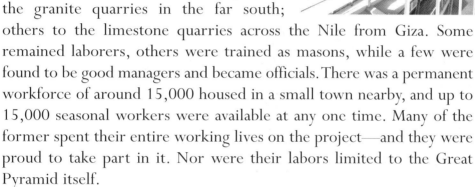

Above: A fanciful Victorian engraving shows the Great Pyramid being used as an observatory by ancient Egyptian priests. Unfortunately, there is no evidence that this was the case.

giant astronomical observatory. This is linked to the more recent suggestions that the pyramid was the creation of some long-lost super-civilization, such as that of the submerged Atlantis, or of visiting aliens from somewhere far off in outer space.

The simple fact is that we just do not know how the ancient Egyptians achieved such a startling degree of mathematical accuracy—but Egyptologists are sure that it was the Egyptians, not anyone else, who achieved it. Nor do we know exactly how the great building blocks were put in place. One theory is that they were dragged on sledges to the site of the pyramid over ground that first had been made slippery. Then, after the first level of blocks was in position, the workers built ramps of mudbrick, limestone chips, and clay, up which blocks for higher levels were pushed and pulled into place. Another popular notion is that the blocks were positioned with the help of long levers with a short angled foot.

What is even more of a mystery, though, is what happened to the treasures that were buried with the pharaohs? No pyramid has ever been found with its contents intact. Egyptologists argue that, despite

Opposite (below): A page from the Book of the Dead *of a man called Hunefer. Such books were collections of spells that the ancient Egyptians placed with their dead to help them through the underworld. Here Hunefer's mummy, supported by a priest or god wearing a jackal mask, is prayed over by three priests. His wife and daughter mourn at his feet.*

"It seemed like a building let down from heaven, untouched by human hands."

GREEK WRITER STRABO, 28 B.C.

all the precautions the pyramid-builders took to conceal tomb entrances and safeguard their contents, many pyramids were looted by grave-robbers. But, at least as far as the Great Pyramid is concerned, the tomb-robber explanation is not supported by hard facts. What we do know is that, at some stage during the pyramid's construction, the decision was made to install a giant red granite sarcophagus in it to house the dead pharaoh's mummified body. Since there was no way of getting the sarcophagus into the existing burial chamber, a new room had to be created higher up, where the sarcophagus could be placed before the chamber walls were built. In addition to the sarcophagus and its

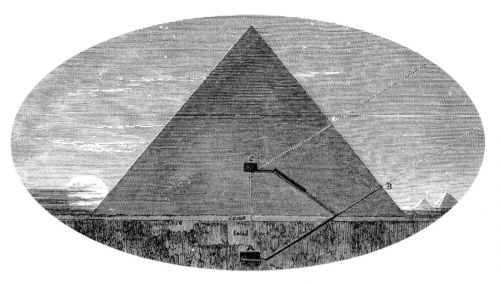

Right: An engraving illustrating Charles Piazzi Smyth's theory that the passageways inside the Great Pyramid were aligned to allow accurate observations to be made of the Pole Star.

Smyth was a reputable 19th-century astronomer, but Britain's Royal Society refused to accept his notions about the pyramids, causing him to resign his membership.

contents, the chamber would have contained furniture, some favorite personal treasures, and what Egyptologists call a canopic chest, which would have held Khufu's embalmed internal organs. So what happened next?

According to history, the first forced entry into the Great Pyramid was made in A.D. 820 by a party of Arab treasure-hunters working for Caliph Abdullah Al Mamoun. Unable to find the builders' hidden entrance, they made their best guess where it might be and spent weeks tunneling into the pyramid's north face. Eventually, they broke through a wall into a descending passage, which they followed down to find the empty, unfinished subterranean chamber and then up to discover the original entrance passage. This was sealed with a granite plug. Undeterred, the caliph and his men hacked through the granite—only to find their way blocked again by a stack of limestone blocks at the start of what is now called the ascending passage. No sooner was one block cleared than another slid forward to take its place. Finally, though, this obstruction, too, was removed, and eventually the group reached the royal burial chamber. There they found nothing but an empty sarcophagus. Even its massive lid had vanished.

So what happened to Khufu's treasures and his mummified remains? If the accounts of Mamoun and his men are to be believed—and what reason did they have to lie?—the stones blocking the only passageways inside the pyramid were still in place when they entered the tomb, and there was no sign of any other disturbance. Therefore the mystery is, if, as many experts suppose, the tomb had been looted, how had the robbers got in and out? Extensive explorations have found no other passageways wide enough to allow for the removal of Khufu's treasures, let alone the sarcophagus's lid.

The speculation is that, perhaps in this case, the pharaoh and his architects managed to outsmart not just the ancient grave-robbers, but also modern Egyptologists. Maybe somewhere in, or below, the last wonder of the ancient world, Khufu still keeps his secrets to himself.

Above: A contemporary depiction of the Battle of the Pyramids (July 21, 1798). When Napoleon invaded Egypt, he took scientists and artists with him. What these French scholars discovered in the sands marked the start of the modern science of Egyptology. Opposite: Higher than a six-story building, the Great Sphinx stands close to the Giza pyramids. It may depict the pharaoh Cephren, or Re-Herakhte, the sun god, but no one knows for sure.

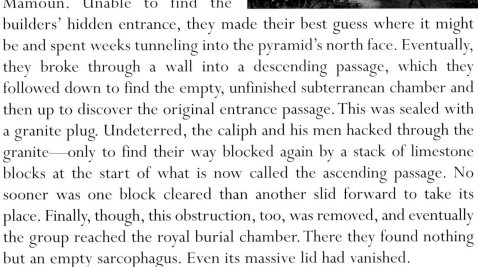

WHO BUILT STONEHENGE AND WHY?

The most famous of all Europe's Stone Age monuments, Stonehenge has always been the subject of intense and sometimes outlandish speculation as to who built it, when, and why. Although modern archaeologists have shed new light on many of the details of its complex story, Stonehenge's true purpose remains unclear. The ancient stones are still wreathed in mystery—a wordless legacy from a time before history began.

Above: Stonehenge's lintels were lowered into place and then fixed by sophisticated joints. In this 14th-century drawing, a craftsman checks the stones' fit.

Viewed from a distance, Stonehenge is more curious than impressive—a jumble of stones in a windswept stretch of the chalk landscape of southern England. Closer up, though, the remnants of order become visible. Uprights and lintels (the horizontal stones) reveal that the jumble is actually a ruin. More details become clear as you approach, and the staggering size of the stones begins to make its impact. They are huge. The largest measure more than 30 feet (just over 9 meters) in length, and weigh more than 44 tons (40 metric tons) apiece.

Most of the stones have fallen, and many have disappeared, probably broken up long ago for use in local building or road construction. But enough stones remain standing for someone visiting Stonehenge today to follow the basic plan. Inside a circular earthwork about 330 feet (100 meters) in diameter, 30 stone uprights and 30 stone lintels once formed a complete inner circle, in the middle of which was a horseshoe arrangement of larger uprights and lintels, now known as trilithons. Various other stones are positioned around the site either alone or in groups. Close inspection reveals that many of the now irregular stones were once carefully shaped and were kept in place by precisely cut tongue-and-groove and mortise-and-tenon joints. Most amazingly, the stone circle was originally a true circle, not a polygon with 30 straight sides—each lintel was slightly curved. Stonehenge was obviously once a very special place, but it is not immediately clear either when or why.

Opposite: Stonehenge has fascinated generations of archaeologists, who have come up with countless fanciful ideas to explain the site's existence. But there is no hard evidence to support their theories that the henge was a center for human sacrifice, that it was used as a giant astronomical calculator, or that it was built by crews of UFOs.

"In archaeology there are always several correct explanations for any set of observed phenomena." ARCHAEOLOGIST STUART PIGGOTT, 1950

For most of early English history, Stonehenge was considered a quaint curiosity. Medieval writers like Geoffrey of Monmouth (c. 1100–55) claimed that either it had been built by a vanished race of giants or that the wizard Merlin had conjured it up by magic. Some modern theorists have come up with equally wild explanations, claiming that UFOs and their alien crews may have been involved in its construction. Though even now some people tend to assume that something as weird and wonderful as Stonehenge must have had a supernatural origin, real history is never quite that simple.

The English writer John Aubrey (1626–97) was one of the first to examine Stonehenge painstakingly. He was a quirky eccentric, fascinated by the antiquities of the English countryside. It was he who discovered a ring of 56 equally spaced pits (now known as the Aubrey Holes) inside the perimeter of the earthwork. Stonehenge also aroused royal curiosity, with King James I (ruled 1603–25) sending his architect Inigo Jones (1573–c. 1652) to view the ruins and give an opinion as to their origin. Jones, who was an ardent student of the classical style of architecture, concluded that the stones were the remains of a temple dating from the time of the Roman occupation (A.D. 43–410). Aubrey, however, disagreed and asserted that the site was pre-Roman, probably built by the British Celts, a tribe who settled in Britain from the 5th century B.C. In the 1740s another English scholar—the antiquarian enthusiast William Stukeley (1687–1765)—wrote yet more about Stonehenge's supposedly Celtic origins. According to Stukeley, Stonehenge was where the Druids, the ancient Celtic priests who had so fiercely resisted the Roman invaders, had conducted their pagan rites and sacrifices. Stukeley published these notions widely, accompanying his writings by lively illustrations, and they captured the public's imagination. As a result, Stonehenge has become closely associated with the revived modern-day Druids—an association for which there is no historical foundation.

Serious study of Stonehenge did not begin until Europe entered the Age of Science in the 19th century, and subsequent investigations have pushed the origins of the monument further and further into the mists of prehistory. Scientific archaeology developed after the Danish

Opposite (top): The 17th-century writer John Aubrey gave his name to the 56 so-called Aubrey Holes, situated just inside the earth bank, which is the earliest portion of the Stonehenge complex. The holes once held wooden posts. It was Aubrey who first made the mistaken connection between the monument and the Druids, an ancient Celtic priesthood that flourished around the time of the Roman conquest (A.D. 43). Opposite (bottom): Druids wearing white robes for holiness and holding a sceptre and crescent, representing the moon. The Druids had little, if anything, to do with Stonehenge. By their time, the monument had been standing for some 2,000 years and was probably in ruins.

Costume of the *Druidical Order.*

Britain	Continental Europe
Nomadic hunter-gatherers move **c.8300** B.C. *into the area we know as Britain.*	
	c.7000 B.C. *Farming spreads from Anatolia (modern Turkey) to southeastern Europe.*
Britain is separated from the **c.6500** B.C. *mainland of Europe when rising sea levels create the English Channel.*	
	c.4700 B.C. *A large stone tomb, the first known stone structure in Europe, is built at Carnac in Brittany, France.*
Farming reaches Britain. The **c.4000** B.C. *earliest known camps and communities appear.*	
Long barrows (stone burial **c.3500** B.C. *chambers covered by mounds of earth) and chambered tombs start to be used for burials around the British Isles.*	**c.3500** B.C. *The temple complex at Tarxien in Malta is built. The wheel is adopted in central Europe.*
	c.3200 B.C. *Stone-circle building is widespread in northwestern Europe.*
Stone circles begin to be **c.3000** B.C. *constructed across Britain. The henge—the circular ditch and bank—is constructed at Stonehenge in Wiltshire.*	**c.3000** B.C *Walled towns emerge in Mediterranean Europe.*
Silbury Hill, Europe's largest **c.2750** B.C. *manmade mound, is constructed near Avebury, Wiltshire.*	
The henge at Avebury, the world's **c.2600** B.C. *most extensive, is constructed.*	
The first stones are brought to **c.2500** B.C. *Stonehenge. Copper-working reaches Britain.*	
	c.2300 B.C. *The European Bronze Age dawns, as evidenced by the appearance of bronze objects in tombs.*
The sarsen stone circle **c.2200** B.C. *is erected at Stonehenge.*	
	c.2000 B.C. *Europe's first advanced civilization, the Minoans, develops on Crete in the Mediterranean: the palace of Knossos is built, Egyptian-influenced hieroglyphs are used, and the potter's wheel is adopted.*
The bluestones are **c.1900** B.C. *brought to Stonehenge.*	
	c.1550 B.C. *The warlike Mycenaeans become the dominant power on the Greek mainland.*
Stonehenge is completed, **c.1500** B.C. *just as stone-circle building seems to be dying out. The wheel finally arrives in Britain.*	
	c.1450 B.C. *The Minoan civilization on Crete is destroyed by a volcanic eruption.*

museum curator Christian Thomsen (1788–1865) divided prehistory into three successive ages—stone, bronze, and iron—on the basis of the materials each used to make tools. First published in 1836, Thomsen's three-age theory gave historians an excellent framework for understanding the distant past. The Society of Antiquaries, in London, began excavating at Stonehenge in 1909, and their investigations suggested that the monument was built in several stages, between

about 1800 B.C. and 1500 B.C., in the middle of the Bronze Age. These dates, however, presented historians with a problem. Although there are many megalithic (from the Greek, meaning "large stone") structures in western Europe, the highly sophisticated upright-and-lintel form of construction used at Stonehenge is unique.

This flew against the prevailing historical theory in the first half of the 20th century, which held that all cultural innovations had a single geographical origin, from which they spread around the world. Archaeologists therefore decided that the craftsmen who built Stonehenge must have come from somewhere other than Britain. The involvement of a Bronze Age architect from the more sophisticated Mediterranean region was suggested accordingly.

This was popularly believed until the invention of radiocarbon dating in the second half of the 20th century. This revolutionized our understanding of prehistory in general, and made it possible to place Stonehenge in the Stone Age once and for all. Stonehenge is 5,000 years old—more ancient than was previously thought possible—and in its earliest form is five centuries older than the pyramids of Egypt. Even more surprisingly, we now know that Stonehenge remained in use for a period of some 1,500 years.

WILTSHIRE.

Above: This attempt to show how Stonehenge might once have looked dates from 1575.

Opposite: By the late 18th century, the link between Stonehenge and the Celtic Druids was established firmly in the public's imagination. The henge was the setting for many copycat festivals. The one shown here was an 1815 Druidic celebration.

"Stonehenge, a Temple restored to the British Druids" — WILLIAM STUKELEY, 1740

The first part to be built was the henge—a circular ditch and bank arrangement—in about 3000 B.C. The Aubrey Holes were dug at the same time or shortly afterward. Some five centuries later, in about 2500 B.C., the first bluestones were brought to the site. These 80 or so stones weigh about 1.6 tons (1.45 metric tons) each. They initially were arranged in two incomplete circles, perhaps in an upright-and-lintel pattern. In about 2200 B.C., Stonehenge underwent

Below: Quite a few of the stones have fallen over time, but modern archaeologists have been able to work out what the site looked like during each stage of its construction.

Opposite: Part of the inner sarsen horseshoe at Stonehenge. The two huge trilithons each consist of a pair of uprights weighing up to 44 tons (40 metric tons) capped by a massive lintel. The smaller bluestones stand in front.

extensive modifications. Large blocks of sarsen stone, averaging 27 tons (24.4 metric tons) each, were quarried from hills 18 miles (29km) away, hauled to the site, and then fitted together to make an unbroken circle. Even larger sarsen blocks were cut and shaped to make the five great trilithons. In about 1900 B.C., the bluestones were rearranged in a spiral outside the sarsen circle, and in about 1500 B.C. they were moved inside the circle. It is the ruins of this final design that visitors see today.

Historians have long since decided against supernatural explanations for the physical construction of Stonehenge. Despite the limitations of technology in the Stone Age, building was really a matter of manpower and human ingenuity. Using stone hammers and wooden rollers and levers, even the largest of the sarsens could have been shaped, transported, and erected by teams of a few hundred workers. The smaller bluestones probably required much less effort. In the 1920s, however, it was suggested that the bluestones had not been collected from the local area around Stonehenge, but instead had been brought from the Prescelli Mountains of southwestern Wales. The geological make-up of the bluestones showed that these were the nearest possible source.

Many people found this difficult to believe and put together an alternative theory: that the bluestones were transported inside glaciers during the Ice Age and deposited in the Stonehenge area when the glaciers melted. Today, though, it is generally accepted that it was human beings who brought the bluestones to Stonehenge. For reasons that are incomprehensible to us 4,000 years later, the people who built the monument shifted more than 132 tons (120 metric tons) of rock more than 125 miles (200km) over land and across the Bristol Channel, between Wales and southwestern England, to arrange them inside a pre-existing henge. The mystery of the bluestones is just a small part of our continuing ignorance about the meaning and purpose of Stonehenge.

The entrance to the original henge was approached by a broad avenue. This avenue was aligned with the direction of the rising sun at the time of the summer solstice, on about June 21, the midpoint of the

solar year. This axis of alignment was maintained throughout the working life of Stonehenge. The apparently important Sanctuary, containing the Heel Stone, was located on this axis, as was the trilithon horseshoe. Alignment with a solstice sunrise is a common feature of megalithic tombs and stone circles in Europe, and may have a deeper significance than merely keeping track of time. The winter solstice, around December 21, marks the start of the solar year, and may have heralded the renewal of the annual farming cycle. In the case of tombs, the alignment may be linked to a belief in rebirth to an afterlife. The summer solstice, at the height of the growing season, was a very important event for farming peoples.

But all this does not explain why Stonehenge had so many different components—the bluestones, the sarsens, the earthwork. An explanation was attempted in the 1960s when Alexander Thom (1894–1985), a professor of engineering at Oxford University, suggested that Stonehenge and other stone circles were in fact astronomical calculators used by Stone Age "scientists" to predict eclipses and tides. According to Thom's theory, the Aubrey Holes at Stonehenge were used for aligning the lunar and solar calendars according to a regular 18.6-year cycle. The theory was "proved" by the discovery through statistical analysis of the "megalithic yard"—an exact standard measurement used for the construction of all stone circles. Unfortunately, with statistics you tend to get what you look for, and the megalithic yard has proved to be a statistical illusion.

What it boils down to is that we know the chronology of Stonehenge, but little else. In about 3000 B.C., farmers dug a ditch and raised a bank to define and enclose a special place. The work was probably a communal effort. It seems likely that this earthen circle was a place of ceremonies or celebrations associated with the farming calendar (contrary to popular belief, there is no evidence that the so-called Slaughter Stone at Stonehenge was ever used for sacrifice—human or otherwise). It also seems probable that the final stages of construction were a prestige project, begun on the initiative of one or more newly important local "cattle barons," who were gaining power through the rearing of cattle.

The best explanation for the structural arrangement of Stonehenge is that it represents a more permanent, stone version of a traditional woodhenge, which had been made up of one or more concentric rings of wooden posts. The woodhenge theory fits the available archaeological facts, but merely rephrases the question because there is no generally agreed explanation for why woodhenges were built by early peoples in the first place. So, although Stonehenge has yielded up some of its secrets, its precise purpose is still a mystery waiting to be solved.

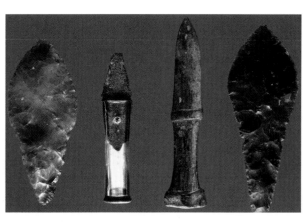

Above: Bronze Age artifacts dredged from stretches of the River Thames in southern England. In the mid-Bronze Age, the construction of Stonehenge was refined by people from this new metal-working culture. Some experts think that they came from mainland Europe, but it is more likely they were British natives.

WAS THERE A TROJAN HORSE?

The tale of the ten-year siege of Troy by the ancient Greeks is one of the most enduring stories in world history. It has captured the human imagination ever since the poet Homer wrote it down. It is also one of the greatest riddles of all time. Is it a myth, as was long believed? Or, as some think, is there now hard evidence to suggest that much of what Homer wrote could be true?

Below: A Roman copy of a 2nd-century B.C. bust of Homer, which is now lost. In reality, no one knows what Homer looked like. Some have even speculated that he was a woman. Opposite: The building of the Trojan horse. According to Homer, the idea for the horse came from Ulysses, the wiliest of the Greek kings.

Today on the site of Troy there stands a giant replica of the fabled Trojan horse. This, according to Homer in *The Odyssey*, was the secret weapon devised by the Greeks to break the stalemate of ten long years of siege and win them final victory in the Trojan War. The story is enchanting. A beautiful Greek queen (Helen) is abducted by a Trojan prince (Paris) and taken back to Troy, which is ruled by his father (Priam). The Greek king (Agamemnon) leads a naval expedition against Troy to retrieve Helen. The conflict lasts a decade, and many heroes, both Greek (Ajax and Achilles) and Trojan (Hector) are involved. The Greeks pretend to depart, leaving behind a wooden horse containing concealed warriors. Despite the warnings of the prophetess Cassandra, the triumphant Trojans take the horse inside the city walls, whereupon the Greeks emerge, sack the city, and put its inhabitants to the sword. It is a masterpiece of storytelling, but is it true?

Homer is a shadowy character. We know little about him—or maybe even her—and all that has survived of his work are two epic poems, *The Iliad* and *The Odyssey*, which were written down in around 730 B.C. (the stories themselves had been oral history for generations). The main reason for the poems' survival is the fact that the Romans, who later conquered the Greeks, fell under the Homeric spell. Indeed, they believed that they themselves were descended from the survivors of Troy, who, fleeing from the fallen city, eventually found refuge in Italy. Though the tale of the Trojan War lived on, classical scholars were unanimous in labeling it a legend.

Even though Homer had included a wealth of detail about Troy and its surroundings in his work, the city's location was unknown to the modern world. The general area was agreed—somewhere near the entrance to the Dardanelles, a strait off the northwestern coast of modern-day Turkey—but

"The seat of sacred Troy is found no more,
No trace of all her glories now remains"

LORD BYRON (1788–1824)

precisely where was anyone's guess. By the mid-19th century the most likely candidate was a low mound at a placed named Hisarlik in Turkey, but there was no actual evidence to prove that this was the case.

In 1871, the German adventurer Heinrich Schliemann (1822–90) began to excavate at Hisarlik. A passionate believer in Homer, Schliemann was an amateur archaeologist and a self-made millionaire. He was impatient and destroyed much of what he discovered through careless technique; he told lies about some of his discoveries; and he illegally smuggled his best finds out of the country. But he did find Troy—or so historians believe.

In fact Schliemann did more than this. What he unearthed was nine separate Troys. Hisarlik is what modern archaeologists call a tell—a mound created by successive layers of settlement—and Schliemann uncovered nine separate levels. The earliest one of which dates back to about 3000 B.C. In level two, Schliemann found his most famous proof for the existence of Troy—a hoard of golden treasure which he claimed had undoubtedly belonged to the Trojan king Priam. He also found evidence that level two had met with the same fate as Homer's city, having been violently destroyed. This was enough to convince Schliemann that what he had found was indeed Homer's Troy.

Later investigations have shown that Schliemann was right overall, but wrong in all-important matters of detail. Level two was too small and too early to have been the "proud towers" besieged by the Greeks. Archaeologists since Schliemann have focused on level six, which is the right age and size to have been Homer's city. Initially, its destruction was attributed to an earthquake, but it is now thought that it could indeed have been caused by a victorious besieging army.

Opposite (top): This medieval illustration shows the wooden horse being pushed into Troy's inner citadel. Obviously, Homeric Troy looked nothing like this, but recent excavation confirms that it was substantially fortified. Opposite (below): Greeks and Trojans battle hand to hand during the siege in this marble relief decorating a Greek sarcophagus.

Greece and Troy		The World	
A settlement grows on the site of Troy.	c.3000 B.C.		
		c.1900 B.C.	The first Chinese city is founded.
The Hittite Empire emerges among the city states of what is now Turkey.	c.1650 B.C.		
The Mycenaeans become the dominant power on the Greek mainland.	c.1550 B.C.	c.1550 B.C.	The nomadic Aryans flood into the Indus Valley and settle northern India.
The Mycenaeans sack Troy.	c.1260 B.C.		
The Hittite Empire falls.	c.1200 B.C.	c.1200 B.C.	The Chavín civilization emerges in modern-day Peru.
Mycenaean Greece collapses.	c.1150 B.C.		
		c.1020 B.C.	Saul becomes the first king of the Israelites.
The first athletics festival is held at Olympia.	776 B.C.		
		753 B.C.	According to legend, Romulus founds Rome.
The Greek alphabet is developed.	c.750 B.C.		
Homer writes down **The Odyssey**.	c.730 B.C.		
		521 B.C.	The Persian Empire stretches from Egypt to the Himalayas.
		510 B.C.	The Romans expel the Etruscans, establishing themselves as a republic.
The Athenians establish a democracy.	505 B.C.		
The Athenians defeat the Persians at Marathon. The rise of the city state of Athens marks the start of the golden age of classical Greece.	c.491 B.C.	c.450 B.C.	The Celts, an Indo-European tribe, reach Britain.
The Spartans defeat the Athenians at Syracuse in Sicily, and become the dominant power in Greece.	413 B.C.	c.400 B.C.	The two great epics of Sanskrit literature, the **Ramayana** and the **Mahabharata**, are written down in India. Hinduism spreads to southern India and Sri Lanka.
Philip of Macedon gains control of Greece.	338 B.C.		
Alexander the Great, Philip's son, starts on his conquest of the Persian Empire, and eventually reaches northwestern India.	333 B.C.		
Alexander the Great dies and his empire dissolves.	323 B.C.		
		c.206 B.C.	The Han dynasty takes control of China, and begins to expand its borders into Central Asia.
Roman forces destroy Corinth, and Greece becomes part of the Roman Empire.	146 B.C.		

Schliemann's discoveries were by no means universally accepted. If Hisarlik was Troy, said the cynics, then what about the enemy? There was no evidence, apart from what Homer had said, that the people who sacked Troy were Greeks. Guided by what Homer had written about Agamemnon's city, Schliemann began excavating at Mycenae in Greece, where he met with spectacular success. He uncovered the remains of a heavily fortified citadel and rich royal graves. He was sure that he had found the palace of Homer's Greek leader. He excavated at other sites and found similar fortifications and further remains. Surely, he thought, this proved that it was ancient Greek warriors who had sailed against Troy. Archaeologists now say that, contrary to opinion at the time, Schliemann's theories appear to have been correct.

Numerous excavations around the Mediterranean have revealed that a seafaring people came to power in Greece around 1550 B.C. After subduing the mainland, the Mycenaeans, as they became known, invaded Crete, where they conquered the great Minoan civilization that was centered on the island. By around 1350 B.C. they had reached the

Left (top): Heinrich Schliemann, discoverer of the remains of Troy. He was inspired to search for the city by the stories his father told him as a child. Left (bottom): His wife, Sophie Schliemann, wears the fabulous golden jewelry that her husband claimed had been part of Priam's treasure and worn by Helen of Troy. Right: Schliemann lecturing on his excavations at Mycenae.

highest point of their power, trading and raiding throughout the eastern Mediterranean region.

These dates in themselves were a compelling reason to believe that the Mycenaeans and Homer's Greeks were one and the same, especially when fragments of Mycenaean pottery were discovered at Troy itself. What many regarded as clinching proof came when the Mycenaean language, samples of which had been found inscribed on clay tablets in a script known as Linear B, was translated. It was unquestionably an early form of Greek. The tablets revealed that the Mycenaeans were warrior slave-owners who kept lists of ships that are remarkably similar to the "List of Ships" enumerated by Homer. As a bonus, archaeologists also unearthed a suit of Mycenaean bronze armor, complete with a boar-tusk helmet. It matched a description in *The Iliad* exactly.

It seemed that there now could be little doubt that the Mycenaeans were Greeks, but, despite the mounting evidence, some scholars continued to minimize the importance of Homer's tale, denying that it corresponded with actual history. Thanks to recent finds, the doubters seem to have been proved wrong. Dr Manfred Korfmann, a German archaeologist who has been directing extensive excavations at Troy since 1988, is convinced that he has found compelling evidence that the city was much larger and more important than previously thought. With an estimated population of up to 10,000—a sizeable one for the time—it was, Korfmann says, a thriving center of late Bronze Age commerce and well worth fighting over. Korfmann believes that Homer's epics have what he terms "an historic core," even though his finds differ from Homer's description in points of detail. Pointing to the extensive fortifications the Trojans built over time and to the city's strategic significance in its control of the shipping routes between the Aegean and the Black Seas, he thinks that there were probably many Trojan Wars, rather than just one. It is these wars, according to Korfmann, that could have served as a basis for Homer's epics.

Korfmann's beliefs, though, are considered controversial by some archaeologists. So, too, are the findings of prominent scholars of Hittite culture Frank Starke and David Hawkins, whose evidence comes from the official archives of the Hittite Empire. The Hittites were a regional superpower based in central Anatolia (Turkey). They were an advanced

Above: The gold funerary mask that Schliemann found at Mycenae and claimed to be that of Agamemnon, ruler of the city and an important leader of the Greeks at Troy. It is as controversial as many other of Schliemann's finds. Some archaeologists claim that Schliemann subtly changed it to prove his point.

"Do not trust the horse you Trojans"

VIRGIL, *THE AENEID*, 19 B.C.

Above: The so-called Lion Gate at Mycenae. It was near here that Schliemann discovered the Mycenaean royal tombs, along with accompanying grave treasures. The city was surrounded by huge walls, except for on the south side, where a ravine provided defensive protection.

civilization that knew when to opt for diplomacy over war. They kept detailed records of their foreign affairs, dating back to the 13th century B.C.

According to Starke and Hawkins, in the northwestern part of the Hittite Empire, close to the entrance to the Dardanelles, was a loyal "client," or economically dependent, kingdom, known as Wilusa. If the W of Wilusa is dropped (the Greeks did not use that letter) then Ilusa is close to Ilium, Homer's alternative name for Troy. The Hittites were also aware of a seafaring people to the west of Wilusa who they called Ahhiyawans, a name similar to Achaeans, Homer's name for the Greeks. Hittite emperors corresponded formally with the ruler of the Ahhiyawans on an equal basis as "brother king."

To add to their evidence, Starke and Hawkins cite a message the Hittite emperor Hattusilias, who ruled at about the time of the destruction of Homeric Troy, sent to the Ahhiyawan king about "the town of Wilusa over which we made war, and over which we have now reached a settlement." The information on the tablets is patchy—with no clues about the causes of the war, the length of the conflict, or the terms of the settlement—but tantalizing nonetheless. It may well represent the official Hittite record of the story that Homer committed to writing some 500 years later.

It is understandable that the Greek and Hittite versions do not mesh exactly. For the Mycenaeans, bloodying the nose of the Hittites was a great victory, to be embellished and exaggerated with every retelling. For the Hittites, the Trojan War would have been no more than a minor irritant, soon smoothed over by the expert hand of imperial diplomacy.

It seems likely, therefore, that there was a Troy, that there was a Trojan War—maybe wars—and that the ancient Greeks were

Below: Roman remains at Troy (c. 27 B.C.– 14 A.D.). Nine successive cities occupied the site, the earliest dating from c. 2920 B.C. Because Heinrich Schliemann believed Homer's Troy must be the oldest on the site, he dug straight through important evidence.

involved. Modern geographical and geological evidence also shows that Homer's description of Troy and the surrounding area is amazingly accurate. What we will never know is whether the war lasted for an epic ten years; whether it was fought for the reasons Homer stated, with the gods and goddesses taking sides, or whether it was simply a battle for commercial supremacy.

What does seem possible, though, is that the notion of the Trojan horse does have a basis in fact, given what we now know of Mycenaean military technology. By the 13th century B.C., wooden siege towers and battering rams had already made their appearance in warfare. In poetic language of the kind favored by Homer, something pushed against the walls of Troy and used to gain entry might easily be called a wooden horse. It was simply Homer's way of spicing up the story. After all, he was a poet, rather than a historian. And it is his work that has kept the tale of Troy and the Trojan Wars alive over the centuries.

Above: The Sanctuary belonging to level eight Troy, close to the west gate. After the fall of level six Troy, historians think the site was not resettled until the time of Alexander the Great. The most recent excavations there started in 1988 and are still continuing.

DID ROME REALLY FALL?

For almost a thousand years, Rome was the world's greatest superpower. Until relatively recently, it was believed that the great civilization then went into a decline, finally meeting a catastrophic end when invading tribes overran the western part of the empire. Now scholars are shedding light on whether or not Rome actually collapsed.

Above: This sculpture is of the hand of Emperor Constantine (ruled A.D. 311–337), a potent symbol of imperial power. According to British historian Edward Gibbon, however, it was Constantine's "feeble policy," including the forced introduction of Christianity as the state religion, that fatally weakened the empire, leading to its "decline and fall."

Just as Rome was famously not built in a day, so the legendary collapse of its empire was not as simple as it seems. Until fairly recently, one thing that historians all agreed on was that Rome did indeed "fall," losing its political power and the control of its vast lands. Across the empire the Romans had built roads and bridges, and imposed order, laws, and a unifying language. The decline of Rome, the historians said, undoubtedly brought an end to civilized life across western Europe, ushering in the so-called Dark Ages that were to last for the next 500 years or so. Now, a fresh look at what actually happened suggests that the effects of Rome's fall had been overdramatized, and that the infamous Dark Ages were not quite as dark as once had been thought.

Many different explanations have been given for Rome's so-called fall. Some say that the decline was the fault of foolish emperors, or of the corruption rife among the Roman people themselves. Others point to overstretched resources, arguing that the empire had simply grown too big to survive. Even the effects of lead poisoning, caused by the pipes the Romans used for their plumbing, have been blamed.

It was the 18th-century British historian Edward Gibbon (1737–94) who penned the classic account of Rome's decline in his massive six-volume survey, *A History of the Decline and Fall of the Roman Empire*. Inspired by the sight of Christian monks praying in what was once the pagan Temple of Jupiter in Rome in 1764, Gibbon started his study in 1772. By the time he published the last three volumes, 16 years and a million and a half words later, his work had won him praise in Europe and America, where none other than the statesman Benjamin Franklin was a fan. On hearing that Gibbon had refused to meet him, the good-natured American quipped that he looked forward to reading Gibbon's *Decline and Fall of the British Empire* some time in the future.

Opposite (top): In this 2nd-century A.D. mosaic, servants and slaves prepare for a decadent Roman feast. Opposite (bottom): A lyre player entertains the dinner guests. By the time of the later emperors, thousands of ordinary Romans were relying on a daily ration of bread, pork, and olive oil doled out by the government, while the wealthy were spending fortunes on all sorts of luxuries. The Romans, it seemed, were starting to prefer good living to facing up to the dangers beginning to threaten their civilization.

"The grandeur that was Rome."

EDGAR ALLEN POE, FROM HIS POEM "TO HELEN," 1848

THE ROMAN EMPIRE
Greatest extent at the time of Trajan, A.D. 117

0 — 400 mi
0 — 400 km

Opposite (top): Though Rome lost its political power well before its fall, it remained the center of the Christian Church for 12 centuries and is still the center of the Catholic faith. The 16th-century St. Peter's Basilica replaced the one built by Constantine in the 4th century. Opposite (bottom): Trajan's Column commemorates one of Rome's greatest emperors, who ruled A.D. 98–117.

What Gibbon said was that there were "four principal causes" for the fall of Rome. These were the ravages of time and nature; internal quarrels; mismanagement of resources; and invasion by barbarian (supposedly less civilized) hordes. No historian has ever challenged Gibbon's devotion in compiling his masterpiece. But, because modern historians have some more reliable sources of information available to them than Gibbon, what they say is that the reasons for Rome's decline and subsequent fall are more complex and varied than Gibbon thought.

Historians now think that Gibbon's first cause was not particularly significant—all peoples and empires have been vulnerable to time and nature. Nor do experts believe the decline was the result of factors like the built-up effects of lead poisoning from the pipes used in Roman plumbing. Even in modern European cities, much of the domestic water supply still passes in part through lead pipes without any ill-effects. As far as Gibbon's second cause is concerned, they point out that, even at the peak of its power, Rome had often been troubled by political splits and yet had managed not just to survive them, but to renew its ambitious imperial expansion after their resolution.

Modern historical opinion, however, is divided about whether Gibbon's third cause holds true. It still has its supporters. Undoubtedly, the Romans were extremely wasteful of their resources. Vast quantities of gold and silver were sent to India and the Orient to pay for luxury imports such as spices and silks. This outflow of wealth persisted for centuries. Add to this the fortune that was being spent on free food allowances for the needy and the unemployed, plus the problems we now know the later emperors had in extracting high taxes from reluctant tax-payers. Perhaps the imperial finances were in trouble.

The contrary argument is that, despite chronic inflation, the Roman economy managed to stay afloat through the development of a token

The Roman Empire		The World	
The Roman Republic is established.	509 B.C.		
		273 B.C.	Ashoka seizes control of the Mauryan throne of India, and begins to expand the empire.
Rome takes control of the whole Italian peninsula.	250 B.C.		
Romans conquer Sicily.	241 B.C.		
		206 B.C.	The Han dynasty takes control of China, and starts a period of dramatic empire expansion.
The Romans defeat Hannibal, the Carthaginian leader, paving the way for expansion into North Africa.	202 B.C.		
The conquest of Greece and North Africa.	146 B.C.		
		c.110 B.C.	The vital Silk Route, linking China with southwestern Asia, is opened up.
Julius Caesar conquers Gallia (modern-day France).	51 B.C.	40 B.C.	Herod the Great becomes king of Judaea (part of Palaestina, or Palestine), which is a client kingdom of Rome.
Egypt falls to Rome's armies.	30 B.C.		
Augustus is the first Roman emperor.	27 B.C.		
Romans conquer Britannia (Britain).	A.D. 43	c. A.D. 30	Jesus dies in Judaea, marking the start of Christianity for his followers.
Paul of Tarsus (in modern Turkey) brings Christianity to Greece.	c.50		
With the conquest of Mesopotamia, the empire is at its largest extent.	117	c.100	The Pyramids of the Sun and Moon are built at Teotihuacán in Mexico.
The assassination of Emperor Commodus sparks years of civil war.	192		
Tribes from Germania start to make inroads into Roman territory.	238	c.250	The Zapotec temple complex is built at Monte Albán in Mexico. Also in Mexico, the Mayan civilization enters its golden age. The first compass is used in China.
Emperor Diocletian creates separate Eastern and Western Roman Empires.	284		
The Edict of Milan promotes Christianity throughout the empire.	313	320	India's golden age begins with the start of the Gupta dynasty.
Emperor Constantine moves his capital to Byzantium and renames the city Constantinople.	330	335	The original Church of the Holy Sepulchre, one of the holiest shrines in Christendom, is completed in Jerusalem.
The Visigoths sack Rome.	410		
Germanic chieftain Odoacer deposes the last emperor of the Western Roman Empire, Romulus Augustulus.	476	475	An incredible 1,600-feet-long keyhole-shaped tomb is completed for Emperor Nintoku of the Japanese Yamato state.

"On every road—death, sorrow, slaughter, fires and lamentation."

ROMAN POET ORENTIUS ON GAUL AFTER THE VANDAL ATTACK OF 406

Left: A 17th-century French woodcut shows the Romans fleeing as the Visigoths led by Alaric sack Rome in A.D. 410. This was not the first time the city had fallen to its enemies. To win peace, Honorius, the western emperor, married his sister to Alaric's successor and granted the Visigoths territories in southwest Gallia (France), where they began to learn Latin and adopt Roman ways. Near right: A few decades later, in A.D. 476, Odoacer, another Germanic chieftain, sacked the city and forced the emperor from his throne.

monetary system. Just as we do today, the Romans paid for things with paper bills and coins rather than with precious metals. In addition, archaeological evidence from the excavations of some late Roman villas—the sort of evidence that was not available to Gibbon—does not suggest that there was a noticeable decline in the Roman standard of living. If Rome was really suffering from a severe and lengthy economic depression, there certainly would be signs of it.

For Gibbon, though, his fourth cause—invasion—was his clincher. Here, the facts seemed straightforward. At the beginning of the 5th century, said Gibbon, the barbarians flooded across the imperial frontiers. The city of Rome was sacked twice, and a German king, Odoacer, finally deposed the last emperor of Rome, Romulus Augustulus, in A.D. 476. With this, Roman civilization in western Europe came to an end and the continent entered the Dark Ages.

In fact, barbarians had threatened Rome before. It had been sacked in 390 B.C. by marauding Celts and had nearly suffered the same fate

again in 116 B.C., when a war-band known as the Cimbri battled their way from the North Sea coast into the heart of the Roman Empire. Not only had large numbers of barbarians crossed the Danube as early as the 3rd century A.D. but they had also been allowed to settle. It seemed as if none of these intrusions had caused Roman power to do anything more than wobble. What, historians asked, made Gibbon's invasions so different?

Part of the answer lay in the arrival of the Huns and the shifts they caused in the balance of power on the barbarian side of the Roman frontiers. The Huns were fierce nomad warriors from the Asian Steppe (vast grasslands east of Sarmatia), where they had long been thorns in the side of the Chinese Empire

Above: From Gallia (France), Alaric and his invading Visigoths moved into Hispania (Spain). Aetius, one of the Western Empire's last capable military leaders, then tried to reassert Roman power. By then, though, many locals preferred rule by the Visigoths to that of Roman governors.

Above: The Roman Forum, with the remains of the Temple of Saturn. The area was the political and economic center of the city until most of it was destroyed by the Visigoths in A.D. 410.

at the far eastern reaches of the continent. For reasons known only to the Huns themselves—perhaps military setbacks, leadership rivalries, or climate change—they began to migrate west, pushing other peoples westward before them. It was like playing dominos—knock one domino in a line over and, one by one, the others topple.

Eventually, Rome was attacked by a kaleidoscope of tribes, including the Huns, who were now organized under the leadership of Attila. The Huns didn't finish the job, though. They were in the process of invading Italy in 453 when their great chief died. Mourning for him, they retreated back to the Steppe. But they left a rapidly disintegrating empire behind them, where some of the other invading tribes were busy setting up new kingdoms of their own. The Vandals, for instance, having cut a path through Gallia, settled in Hispania (Spain), until another tribe, called the Visigoths, forced them across into North Africa.

"And when Rome falls—the World"

BRITISH POET LORD BYRON (1788–1824), *CHILDE HAROLD'S PILGRIMAGE*

So far so good, say present-day historians, but there was another side to the story. This makes it even more complex—and even more fascinating. Rome, it now seems, was not simply toppled by barbarians. In fact, the city, along with much of the empire in the west, was actually sacrificed by some of those in power—just like a chess player on occasion may sacrifice pieces in order to stay in and win the game.

It was back in the heyday of their empire that the Romans set deliberate limits on their European expansion. So Hadrian's Wall in Britannia (England) marked the northern boundary of the empire, while heavily defended fortifications were built along the Rhine and Danube Rivers. The idea was that these frontiers would be easily defensible. Later, a series of rebellions and invasions convinced the empire's rulers that this policy was no longer working. Instead, the Romans developed a sophisticated system of defense "in depth," leaving

Above: The House of
the Vestals (seen on
the left) in the
Roman Forum. This
was the home of the
Vestal Virgins, the
priestesses of the
goddess Vesta. Other
important buildings
in the area included
the Curia, where the
Senate met in debate.

the actual frontiers only lightly manned. The emphasis was now on mobility, with the best troops being held back to deal with raids when they actually took place. Eventually, though, the system broke down in the face of the sheer number of invasions, and the Roman commanders were forced to choose which portions of the empire to defend. They chose to sacrifice the west, including Rome itself.

There was more to this decision than simple military logic. Its roots go further back—to the time when Roman rulers began to realize that their empire had become simply too big and too complex to have a single capital and a single monarch. Their solution was simple. They split the empire in two, with an eastern capital at Byzantium (which later became Constantinople and is now Istanbul), a western one at Rome, and joint emperors, one ruling the east and the other the west. From the end of the 4th century, the west was abandoned by the much

"After diligent enquiry I can discern four principal causes of the ruin of the Roman Empire."

EDWARD GIBBON, 1776

wealthier east. The importance of Rome diminished. It was not even the capital of the Western Empire—most of the later emperors preferred to rule their dominions from the Italian cities of Mediolanum (Milan) or (Rauenna) Ravenna. So, when Rome itself was sacked by Odoacer, the importance of the event, many scholars now say, was more symbolic than real.

As for the rest of the Western Empire, some modern historians argue that the fall of Rome marked no more than a handover of the administrative reins of power, both in the city and across the empire. They claim that, contrary to belief, the coming of the "barbarians" did not bring any marked changes with it. Christianity, which—rather than paganism—had been the official religion of the empire since 313 A.D., had spread far beyond the imperial frontiers long before the barbarians arrived. The "fall" brought no mass shift back to pagan ways. King Odoacer himself was a Christian, as were the Visigoths who sacked Rome in 410. In 498 the Franks, who settled in what is now northern France, converted to Christianity.

Nor were the majority of ordinary people that greatly affected. Across much of western Europe, according to archaeological evidence, life under the barbarians was little different than life during the final years of the Roman Empire. The people who did suffer were the members of the previously wealthy Roman governing class. Those who remained in the west were deprived of most of their property and forced to serve the new barbarian rulers. Others fled to the east.

What historians now think is that, rather than asking why the Roman Empire fell, it is more fascinating to speculate on why so much managed to survive. The fallen empire left behind it the foundations upon which medieval Christendom and modern Europe were built. In terms of language, laws, religion, and more, much of the Roman achievement survived. In that sense the Romans built—better than they knew—what turned out to be a legacy for all time.

Top left: Gold and silver coins were essential ingredients of empire. Some historians say that inflation contributed to the empire's problems. Above: Remnants of Roman rule stand as far away as Jerash in Jordan. Opposite: At the other end of the empire, Hadrian's Wall, built to protect the border of the empire in Britain, still snakes its way across the countryside.

WAS THERE A REAL KING ARTHUR?

King Arthur is a mysterious figure, and his tale has a long and complex history. Writers from every age have constructed their own version of Arthur, tailored to suit the spirit of their times. But was there a real King Arthur? If so, exactly who was the historical figure behind the folk tale? How did the world-famous legend emerge? It is one of history's greatest unsolved riddles.

Left: This picture of King Arthur, complete with a shield upon which the Virgin Mary and the baby Jesus are depicted, was drawn around the year A.D. 1300 to illustrate a contemporary chronicle. The armor Arthur is wearing in the depiction is totally medieval. Even if he had existed, he would never have been dressed like this.

Almost everyone has heard of King Arthur. He was the ancient British king who pulled the sword from the stone, consulted the magician Merlin, led the knights of the Round Table, married the beautiful Guinevere, counted Sir Lancelot among his most loyal followers, and set an example of bravery and chivalry for friend and foe alike. According to British legend, though he is long dead, he lies somewhere in the hills, waiting for the moment when his countrymen need him most. Then he will awake and save them.

Is this history? Much of it certainly is not. The magical Merlin sounds suspect, and how could a sword possibly be embedded in a stone in the first place? That all sounds like folklore. But just because the story is folklore now does not necessarily mean that it did not have a historical seed. It is for that seed that historians and archaeologists have long been looking.

A historian usually starts by looking for written evidence. The first mention of someone who might be Arthur is in a book called *The Overthrow of Britain* compiled by the British monk Saint Gildas (c. A.D. 516–70). In this book, a British leader named Ambrosius slows the advance of the invading Angles and Saxons, who are later defeated at the Battle of Mount Badon in about 500. Gildas does not mention Arthur, nor say that Ambrosius fought at Badon, but some historians have wondered if Ambrosius and Arthur are one and the same. This is historical evidence, but was it Arthur?

Right: According to legend, Arthur established his right to kingship by pulling a sword from the stone in which it had been embedded by the wizard Merlin. It may be that the story came about because some early chronicler miscopied "saxo," the Latin word for stone, for "Saxon:" it is far more probable that Arthur slew a powerful Saxon leader and took his sword as a war trophy.

"Whoso pulleth out this sword of this stone and anvil is rightwise King born of all England."

THOMAS MALORY, *MORTE D'ARTHUR*, 1485

Above: Lancelot of the Lake kneels to receive his spurs of knighthood, watched by the ladies of Arthur's court. The woman dressed in blue could be Guinevere. However, there is absolutely no evidence that Lancelot or anyone like him ever existed. He was entirely the invention of the medieval French writer Chrétien de Troyes.

At the same time, bards in Wales and Brittany, in France, were entertaining their hosts with stories of a hero named Arthur. This one had a personality much like that of the Arthur we know, and he slew monsters and wicked giants. Folk heroes are sometimes based on history. But was this Arthur real?

The next piece of written evidence comes from the early 9th century, when Arthur was named by the Welsh monk Nennius in his *History of the Britons*. According to Nennius, Arthur was a British war leader who fought a series of 12 battles against the Angles and Saxons, of which Badon was the last. The similarities with Ambrosius are unmistakable.

And that, together with poems and a few other writings of the same time, is all of the written evidence we have for King Arthur. All of the details—Lancelot, Guinevere, the sword in the stone, Camelot and the Round Table, Merlin the magician—appear only in literature, much of it written long after the Norman Conquest of 1066. Such Arthur stories started in 1139, when a chronicler called Geoffrey of Monmouth (c. 1100–55) published his *History of the Kings of Britain*. In France, the story was taken up by poets such as Chrétien de Troyes (died c.1185). And probably the most famous version of all—Sir Thomas Malory's *Morte D'Arthur*—was published as late as 1485.

For hundreds of years after that, people were content to leave Arthur as a legend. Then, in the early 20th century, some historians began to wonder. Could Arthur possibly be real after all? One popular view held by many scholars was that Arthur was actually a late-Roman cavalry commander who had led British forces against the invading Anglo-Saxons. The theory came from an exact interpretation of Nennius's Latin description. He called Arthur a "*dux bellorum,*" a specific late-Roman military rank. Other historians are not so sure. They wonder if Nennius, writing nearly 400 years after the Roman withdrawal from Britain, could have known about the specialized Roman use of the term. Maybe he was simply using it literally, since translated it means "war leader."

Archaeologists have also been looking around Britain for evidence of the real Arthur. One such investigation took place in 1976 in the city of Winchester in southern England, where, in the Great Hall of

Opposite (top): In this French medieval illustration, Lancelot (far right) goes to the aid of Guinevere (not pictured), who has been carried off by bandit knights. Lancelot, according to Chrétien de Troyes, was skilled in all the arts that made a knight successful: arms, chivalry, and the art of courtly love. But it was his love for the queen that proved to be his undoing. Opposite (below): Sir Gawain presents himself to Arthur and Guinevere. As in the case of Lancelot, there is no reason to suppose that Gawain ever existed outside the pages of literature.

Britain		The World	
Tribes of Angles, Saxons, and Jutes start to flood into Britain.	c.390		
The Romans abandon Britain.	410	*St. Patrick arrives in Ireland, bringing Christianity with him.*	432
Ambrosius, a Christian Romano-British leader, makes a last stand against an army of invading pagan Saxons at the Battle of Mount Badon.	c.500		
The monk Gildas mentions Ambrosius in **The Overthrow of Britain.**	c.547	*Buddhism reaches Japan. Ethiopian monks translate the Bible.*	c. 540
St. Augustine is sent by Pope Gregory I to convert the Anglo-Saxon kings of England to Christianity.	597	*Mohammed is born in Mecca.*	570
The Isle of Wight (off southern England) is the last part of Anglo-Saxon England to be converted to Christianity.	687	*A series of Islamic conquests begins with the taking of Mesopotamia.*	637
		Ancestors of the Maori reach New Zealand.	c.700
Ethelbald takes the crown of Mercia and dominates most of England, as overlord of the Anglo-Saxon kingdoms.	716	*Muslim forces cross the Straits of Gibraltar and conquer Spain.*	711
The earliest known Viking raid (of Danes and Norwegians) takes place.	787	*The center of the powerful Arab world is the Abbasid Caliphate at Baghdad.*	762
An army of Danes moving across England is defeated by Alfred the Great of Wessex. Nennius names King Arthur as the hero of the Battle of Mount Badon in his **History of the Britons.**	c. 870	*Charlemagne, king of the Franks, is crowned Holy Roman Emperor. His lands cover much of Europe.*	800
		Arab mathematicians invent the concept of zero.	873
England is split between Danish territory to the east (the Danelaw), and Anglo-Saxon land to the west.	886	*The Vikings (Norsemen) found the duchy of Normandy.*	911
King Swein of Denmark forces all of England to submit to him. The Anglo-Saxon King Ethelred flees to Normandy.	1013	*Christians begin to reconquer Spain.*	1031
		Macbeth becomes king of Scotland, after murdering Duncan.	1040
Edward, son of Ethelred, returns from Normandy and takes the throne.	1042	*Printing with movable type is invented in China.*	1045
Harold Godwinson, the last Anglo-Saxon king, loses the Battle of Hastings to the invasion force of Duke William of Normandy.	1066		

Winchester Castle, there hangs an enormous round table-top. It is made of solid oak, is 18 feet (5.4 meters) in diameter, weighs one-and-a-quarter tons (1,138 kilograms) and has places for 25 people marked on it. Many argued that it was the actual Round Table of legend. Historically, Winchester had become the capital of the Saxon kings of Wessex in the 7th century. Could the Saxons possibly have turned Arthur's capital into their own?

Unfortunately, the belief did not stand up to modern scientific investigation. Tree-ring and radiocarbon dating, plus a study of medieval carpentry practices, revealed that the table was actually constructed in the 1270s at the start of Edward I's reign. This was during a time when the king himself was taking a great interest in everything associated with Arthur. He even made the long journey to

Above: Tintagel Castle, Cornwall, is where, according to Geoffrey of Monmouth, Arthur was born. Though the actual ruins are medieval, excavations have shown that in the 400s and 500s the site was the center of a prosperous kingdom.

Glastonbury to be present at the reburial in a splendid new tomb of what were claimed to be Arthur's and Guinevere's bones. The table at Winchester, the experts now think, was probably made to be used at the many knightly tournaments that Edward himself liked to hold.

Although no genuine Arthurian objects have ever been discovered—or have not survived if they have—many possible Arthurian places have been investigated. Geoffrey of Monmouth said that Tintagel in Cornwall was Arthur's birthplace, and there is even a suitably ruined castle perched on a cliff there. But, unfortunately, the castle is no older than Geoffrey himself. There are, however, traces of earlier settlements beneath the castle walls, so it is possible that people did live there in Arthur's time. But any hard evidence linking Arthur himself with Tintagel is lacking. Writers choose places as settings for their books for many different reasons. Geoffrey may have inserted the reference to Tintagel simply to please a rich local nobleman.

Many believe that the ancient site of Glastonbury is the Isle of Avalon, where Arthur and Guinevere supposedly were buried. The roots of this story can be dated precisely to 1191, when the monks of Glastonbury Abbey uncovered what they claimed to be the graves of Arthur and his queen. From Arthur's supposed grave, they recovered a cross inscribed with the Latin words "*Hic lacet sepultus inclytus Rex Arthurius in Insula Vallonia cum uxore secundus Wenneveria*" ("Here lies the renowned King Arthur in the Isle of Avalon with his second wife Guinevere"). On digging further, the monks found a hollow tree trunk containing the bones of what appeared to be an immensely tall man, plus some smaller bones and a scrap of hair. The man's bones bore the marks of ten wounds, all of which had healed except for one. Unfortunately, the remains

Above: A 14th-century illustration of King Arthur's Round Table. Sir Thomas Malory claimed that there were 150 Knights of the Round Table, but the notion was a medieval invention. The idea was to create a legendary knightly order that would epitomize all the prized qualities of chivalry—courage, honor, dignity, courtesy, nobility, and religious faith. Arthur and his knights, it was claimed, protected the weak, honored and fought for justice, and undertook all kinds of perilous adventures.

Below: In early times, it is likely that Glastonbury Tor, in Somerset, was surrounded by water. This led to its identification as the Isle of Avalon, where Arthur is supposed to lie buried. However, the medieval monks of nearby Glastonbury Abbey claimed to have uncovered and reburied his bones.

Above: Episodes in the life of King Arthur, from a 13th-century French manuscript. The most popular view today is that Arthur, if he existed, was not a king at all. It is more likely that he was a professional soldier—a brilliant military leader employed by an alliance of British rulers to lead their forces against incoming enemies. It was Geoffrey of Monmouth who awarded him the title High-King of Britain.

disappeared when King Henry VIII ordered the Abbey's closure in 1539. As for the cross, it survived until around 1720, when it mysteriously vanished from nearby Wells Cathedral, where it had been housed.

So the claims of the monks cannot be substantiated. In medieval times, monasteries like the one at Glastonbury often relied on visitors for additional income—and the monks needed extra funds to pay for their abbey's rebuilding after it was destroyed by fire a few years before. An attraction such as the remains of the legendary Arthur and Guinevere certainly would have boosted tourism.

Then there is Camelot, Arthur's fabled court, which has held its place as a cornerstone in the Arthurian story ever since a French poet invented the name in the 12th century. The search for Camelot's location rages on. Geoffrey of Monmouth suggested that Arthur's court was on the site of the Roman fortress at Caerleon, in southern Wales. Despite the presence of a "round table" in the form of a ruined amphitheater, the notion that Caerleon was Camelot has been generally discredited because no other supporting evidence has been found.

In the 1960s, the search for Camelot heated up when archaeologists excavated an Iron Age hill fort at Cadbury Castle in southern England. Local legend held that Arthur and his knights lay sleeping under the hill, while John Leland, a historian writing during King Henry VIII's reign, had stated that the local people often referred to the fortified remains as "Camalat—King Arthur's palace."

Exhaustive excavations conducted by the archaeologist Leslie Alcock yielded evidence dating from about Arthur's time of a wall encircling an extensive hilltop compound. At its center was a large aisled hall. The interpretation of these findings is controversial. Where some see the remains of a stout defensive wall around a great feasting hall such as might befit a king named Arthur, skeptics see only a moderately sized barn surrounded by walls barely able to contain horses and cattle, let alone keep determined enemies at bay.

So King Arthur remains a mystery. Though archaeologists can find no evidence for Arthur, this fact alone does not disprove his existence. Archaeologists are the first to explain that lack of proof is not a

Below: The Lady of the Lake reclaims Excalibur, Arthur's enchanted sword, in this 1893 illustration by Aubrey Beardsley. By this time, history had long been abandoned in favor of magical fables, legend, and romances.

convincing argument against the existence of a person, place, or event. All it takes is one small piece of evidence—one small "voice"—to overcome the accumulated weight of silence. Such a discovery may well lie in the future.

But there is another Arthurian mystery. Why is it that we so much want King Arthur to be real? Why do historians and archaeologists continue this search? One of the great attractions of the Arthur story is that it contains something for everyone—action, mystery, romance, the struggle between good and evil. And the tales have a ring of truth because some have their roots in genuine ancient traditions. One example is the story of Excalibur's return to the Lady of the Lake.

Above right: The search for the Holy Grail is an enduring Arthurian myth. Here, Arthur and his knights watch one of their number swear an oath before starting on the quest.

Archaeologists have now discovered that in the Bronze Age (1,000 years before Arthur) it was common practice to ritually "sacrifice" swords by throwing them into water. Who is to say that Arthur's tale does not preserve authentic scraps of belief from much earlier times?

And the idea of a once and future king, sleeping somewhere, awaiting his time to return, is not unique to the Arthur story. In Denmark, the knight Holger Danske sleeps; in Spain it is El Cid; in Germany, Frederick Barbarossa. Arthur embodies real human needs and desires. We *want* him to be real.

WHAT HAPPENED TO THE KNIGHTS TEMPLARS?

Over their 200-year existence, the Knights Templars acquired great power and wealth. Then, early in the 14th century, they were brutally suppressed. Had they really been devil-worshipping heretics as was alleged, or were they the innocent victims of greedy rivals? Did they hide a vast fortune and survive as a secret organization, to emerge centuries later under a new banner? Speculation over what could have happened to this mysterious brotherhood continues today.

Above: A Knight Templar in traveling dress. Though the knights of the order took vows of poverty, they soon became wealthy and powerful. They established themselves as moneylenders to the monarchs of Europe, while legally they were exempt from any authority save that of the popes.

In the Crusades of the Middle Ages an aggressively Christian Europe mounted a series of invasions of the Holy Land. The twin aims were to take the area from its Muslim rulers and to protect Christian pilgrims. Jerusalem fell to the invading Christians in 1099 during the First Crusade. As the Crusaders became established in Palestine, groups of deeply devout fighting knights banded together under monastic rules to form what became known as the military orders. Some knights had been informally protecting pilgrims to the Holy Land for several years by this time, but it was not until 1119 that the Knights Templars officially incorporated themselves into a military order for the defense of Jerusalem and the protection of Christian pilgrims making the hazardous journey from the Mediterranean port of Acre to the city. King Baldwin II of Jerusalem gave the order his blessing and provided them with lodgings in his palace on the supposed site of the famous biblical Temple of Solomon. From this, the order took its name, "les pauvres chevaliers du temple" (Poor Knights of the Temple).

From these modest beginnings, the Templars rapidly became one of the wealthiest and most powerful institutions in the medieval world. Estimates of Templars numbers vary, but at their 13th-century peak there may have been as many as 20,000 of them. They were ferocious in battle, and, at least in their early years, combined this martial valor

Opposite: The recapture of Jerusalem by the charismatic Muslim leader Saladin in 1187 marked the turning point in Christian fortunes in the Holy Land. Saladin was one of the greatest military leaders the Islamic world ever produced. He was also amazingly humane. Unlike the Crusaders, he refused to slaughter those of other faiths.

"*They go into war to fight, and return in peace to rest and to take time to pray: so that they are knights in battle, and like monks at home.*"

JACQUES DE VITRY, BISHOP OF ACRE 1216–28,
ON THE KNIGHTS TEMPLARS

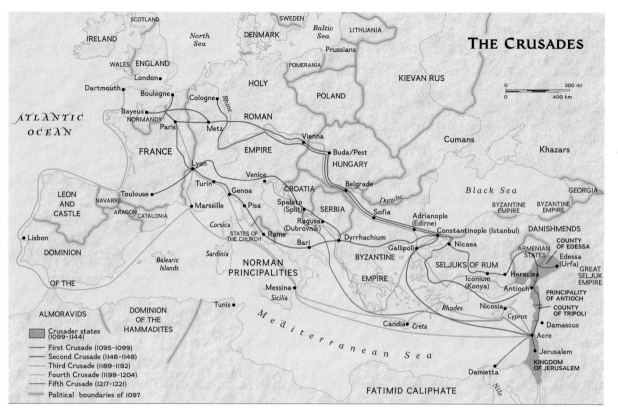

THE CRUSADES

with a piety befitting their dual identity as warrior-monks. They were widely admired for representing an ideal of Christian conduct, and the ecclesiastical and secular authorities competed with each other to shower them with favors and privileges. These included freedom from taxation, plus various legal rights, as well as the gifts of great estates from devout benefactors all over Europe, but especially France.

The unique combination of the Templars' wealth, the sanctuary of their vast estates and safe houses spanning Europe and the Middle East, and their ability to provide travelers with physical security, gave them enormous influence over the commercial life of the time. When money was lodged with them, they would issue letters of credit, which could be redeemed elsewhere in their unofficial empire, in effect making the Templars Europe's first bankers. This brought even more money cascading into their coffers. By the late 13th century, the Templars negotiated as equals with Europe's greatest kings and princes, and acknowledged allegiance only to the pope.

It was now, however, that the tide of events began to turn against the great Knights Templars. The Muslim Saracens, led by Saladin, recaptured

Opposite (top): The Knights Templars made their headquarters in Jerusalem, but were expelled when the city fell to the Muslims. Wave upon wave of Crusaders then tried to reconquer the holy city. Opposite (center): Frederick II and his army arrived in the Holy Land equipped with siege towers and bridges, but the wily emperor won the right to reoccupy Jerusalem in 1229 through diplomacy, not war. Opposite (bottom): The Templars also turned to diplomacy, advocating an alliance with the Muslims of Damascus against the Egyptian Mamluks, but it was the latter who took Jerusalem in 1244, putting its people to the sword.

The Crusades		The World	
Jerusalem, a holy city to Muslims, Jews, and Christians, is taken by the Seljuk Turks, and Christians are denied access.	1071		
		1085	The Domesday Book, *a comprehensive land survey, is compiled in England.*
Pope Urban I calls on Christian Europe to free the Holy Land from the "infidel" Muslims.	1095		
The poor, promised privileges, are the first to set off, sacking cities on the way.	1097	1098	*The Cistercian monastery at Cîteaux, France, is founded. The Cistercians' developments in farming advance European agriculture.*
The First Crusade reaches the Holy Land. Jerusalem is captured, and Jews and Muslims are massacred. Four feudal Crusader states are set up: Jerusalem, Antioch, Edessa, and Tripoli.	1099	c.1100	*The Anasazi of southwest North America build fortified cliff dwellings at Mesa Verde. The Toltecs set up their capital at Tula in Mexico.*
The Knights Templars form a military order, entrusted with the defense of the Crusader states.	1119	1121	*Bishop Eirik of Greenland apparently visits "Vinland," or North America.*
Edessa falls to the Muslims.	1144		
The Second Crusade is defeated.	1147	1147	*Lisbon is taken from the North African Moors.*
Jerusalem is retaken by the Muslims, led by Saladin, who fails to seek revenge for the earlier Crusader bloodbath.	1187		
Richard the Lionheart of England leads the Third Crusade, but turns back partly because his brother John is intriguing against him at home.	1191	1191	*The Zen Buddhist order is founded in Japan.*
Richard is shipwrecked and then captured by Austrians on the way home. His ransom nearly bankrupts England.	1192	1192	*The Afghan Ghurids defeat the Hindu Rajputs of India.*
		1211	*The Mongols start their conquest of China, led by Genghis Khan.*
Emperor Frederick II makes a settlement that wins back control of Jerusalem.	1229		
The last Christian toehold in the Holy Land is lost.	1291		
		1306	*Philip the Fair expels all Jews from France.*
Philip the Fair orders the arrest of all the Templars in France.	1307		
The pope formally dissolves the order of Knights Templars.	1312		
		1314	*The English are defeated by the Scots at Bannockburn.*

"In this religious order has flourished and is revitalized the order of knighthood."

PROLOGUE TO THE *RULE OF THE TEMPLARS*, 1129

Opposite: Acre, one of the major cities of the Holy Land, fell to the Crusaders in 1191 after a two-year siege. Here, Philip Augustus of France leads his knights in an attack on the Muslim garrison. After the victory, the Knights Templars played a major role in holding the city for Christianity. When it was finally recaptured by the Muslims a century later, many chroniclers said that the reason for its loss was the death of William of Beaujeu, the Grand Master of the Templars.

Jerusalem in 1187. The Templars were able to hold Acre for a further century, but, when that last toehold in Palestine fell in 1291, every Christian warrior who got into Muslim hands was put to the sword. Those Templars who survived the massacre at Acre took refuge in Cyprus, from where they hoped—in vain—eventually to mount a counterattack.

Eviction from the Holy Land may have removed the original purpose of the Templars but, with their organizational and financial headquarters in Paris, they still seemed unassailable as an institution. That sense of security was an illusion, however. An organization as rich as the Templars inevitably became the target of resentment. In their later years they had gained a widespread reputation for arrogance; for behaving as though their wealth and privileges made them a law unto themselves. This meant that, when they found themselves under threat, there were few willing to come to their aid. This threat came in the form of a flurry of allegations that the secret initiation rituals of the order were literally diabolical—that the Templars were in fact sworn enemies of Christ and, according to the most lurid charges, were active worshippers of Satan. In an age as intensely focused on salvation and damnation as medieval Europe, there could be no graver accusations.

Leading the attack on the Templars was Philip the Fair, king of France. When he failed to persuade Pope Clement V, the recently elected head of the Church, that the accusations of heresy and depravity required investigation, he took matters into his own hands. On October 13, 1307, in a swoop worthy of a modern security service, Philip had all the Templars in France arrested. The pope protested against this on the grounds that he alone had jurisdiction over the Templars, but to no avail. Under torture and threat of torture, many of the knights confessed to profanities like spitting on the crucifix, and to homosexual acts that at that time were regarded as abominations. Even the Grand Master of the Templars, Jacques de Molay, admitted to sacrilegious behavior.

Above: The crowning of Pope Clement V in Avignon, France, in 1305. A weak man who was firmly under the thumb of Philip the Fair, Clement was quick to fall in with the king's plans.

Above: Philip the Fair of France pictured on a gold coin, carrying his scepter in his left hand and the fleur-de-lys, symbol of the French monarchy, in his right. Philip feared the Templars because of their power and their immunity from royal authority. He also needed their vast wealth to finance the war he was waging against Edward I of England.

Pope Clement was skeptical about the validity of such confessions. In June 1308, however, 72 of the "guilty" Templars repeated their confessions to his face. Clement was then obliged to order a papal commission to investigate the order, not just in France but throughout Europe. Whether torture was employed or not varied from time to time and place to place. The investigations dragged on for years and, not surprisingly, torture and the threat of torture prompted more confessions than did simple questioning. No other investigations produced such startling revelations of corrupt practices as those that took place in France.

However, the situation in France became clouded when many who had confessed under torture retracted. Those who did so were accused of relapsing into heresy and were then handed over to the secular authorities—which put them at Philip's mercy. Of that there was none, and in May 1310, 54 Templars were burned at the stake. Four years later, Jacques de Molay decided he could live no longer with his own forced confession and denounced the allegations as a tissue of lies. On March 18, 1314, he went to the stake outside Notre Dame Cathedral in Paris. According to legend, as the flames consumed him he was heard to summon the king and pope to join him at the bar of heavenly justice. Both King Philip and Pope Clement were dead within the year.

Molay's death symbolized the end of the Templars, but in fact the pope had formally dissolved the order two years earlier, in 1312. In Christian Spain and Portugal, remnants of the Templars were allowed to carry on under new names, but elsewhere they disbanded and their possessions were confiscated and handed over to a rival order, the Knights Hospitaller. In France and England the ruling monarchs managed to get hold of most of the knights' property.

With their departure from the historical stage, the Templars enter the shadowy world of mystery, myth, and conjecture. Whether or not they were guilty has been debated endlessly. Their defenders point out that Philip the Fair was notoriously grasping. Coveting the Templars' wealth, he took advantage of Clement's weakness to bring about their downfall. On this reading, the Templars were innocent martyrs. On the other side, some have always argued strongly that behind the Templars there lay a deep conspiracy to subvert Christianity, and in particular the

Opposite: Jacques de Molay, Grand Master of the Order of the Knights Templars, faces arrest in October 1307, shortly after being summoned to France by Philip the Fair and Pope Clement V. Shortly before, de Molay had been made godfather to Philip's son, perhaps to allay any suspicions he might have had of the king's intentions.

"Therefore, with a sad heart . . . we suppress, with the approval of the sacred council, the order of Templars, and its rule, habit, and name, by an inviolable and perpetual decree."

POPE CLEMENT V'S PAPAL BULL DISSOLVING THE KNIGHTS TEMPLARS IN 1312

> *"To say that which is untrue is a crime both in the sight of God and man. Not one of us has betrayed his God or his country."*
>
> JACQUES DE MOLAY BEFORE HE WAS BURNED AT THE STAKE IN 1314

Above: French royal officials arrested all the Templars in the kingdom on the same day. And where France led, the rest of Europe followed.

Roman Catholic Church. Some even argue that this conspiracy continues to this day among the Freemasons, who—like the Templars—perform secret initiation rites. The fact that some (but by no means all) Freemasons claim at least spiritual kinship with the Templars is held to reinforce that suspicion. A more balanced view is that individual Templars undoubtedly abused their position (which is probably inevitable in any organization that became as large as the Templars), and that some few may have indulged in dubious initiation rites.

More intriguing is the fate of the Templars' fortune. While their estates were forfeited, it is said that a vast hoard of treasure was spirited out of Paris on the fateful day of the mass arrest and taken to the Atlantic port of La Rochelle. From there, some say that a Templar fleet spirited it away to some secret hiding place that has never been found. With this fortune, surviving Templars were able to set up an underground organization that eventually emerged into the open as the international society of Freemasons.

As to where the treasure was hidden, the theory suggests that the fleeing Templars made their way to Scotland, where they were given sanctuary by Robert Bruce, king of the Scots, who was battling to preserve Scottish independence against Edward I of England. In 1314 he led the Scots to a stunning victory at the Battle of Bannockburn, where against overwhelming odds he routed Edward's son and successor Edward II. According to the theory it was the Knights Templars, the most feared cavalry in Europe, who turned the tide for Robert Bruce at Bannockburn.

The theory then extends the Scottish link to the emergence of Freemasonry in Scotland at the beginning of the 17th century. The story picks up again at the end of the 1700s, when traces of a carefully hidden treasure cache were stumbled upon in out-of-the-way Oak Island, in Nova Scotia, Canada. The hiding place—if that is what it is—has

Right: This narrative illustration tells the story of the destruction of the Knights Templars and the subsequent death of Philip the Fair. The king's funeral bier is visible to the lower left. Far right: After six years in prison, Jacques de Molay was burned at the stake after retracting his confessions, which he said he made "through the pain of torture and the fear of death."

become famous as the Money Pit, a deep well that seems to have been cunningly constructed so that it floods whenever attempts are made to get to the bottom of it. Some claim that it contains pirate loot. But others point out that Nova Scotia means New Scotland, so just maybe Oak Island was the final destination of the Templars' treasure.

What the fabled treasure actually consisted of has been the subject of just as much speculation. Some have suggested that the early Templars uncovered priceless relics in Jerusalem—the Ark of the Covenant and the Holy Grail among their number. But if the treasure really contained such artifacts, the question surely is why the Templars, or the Freemasons, never revealed them. Others believe the treasure consists of purely worldly wealth, but on a scale so colossal as to defy imagining. Whatever the truth, the story of the Templars, their treasure, and their fate is still likely to inspire controversy for years to come.

WAS MARCO POLO A GREAT EXPLORER OR A LIAR?

When Marco Polo returned to Venice after 24 years' absence in the East, few believed the tales he told of his travels. But over the years, they became generally accepted as a true record. Now, the controversy has resurfaced and many modern scholars are certain that Polo never visited China at all. What's the true story?

Above: A 15th-century manuscript illustration of a scene in Marco Polo's Il Milione. *It shows a mason and carpenter at work, a shopkeeper serving a customer, and herdsmen driving swine. One of the most powerful arguments for the book's authenticity is the amount of detail it goes into about everyday affairs.*

According to a story circulated by the Dominican friar Jacopo d'Acqui some years after Marco Polo's death in 1324, the famous Venetian merchant and traveler to China was asked on his deathbed to repudiate the "many great and strange things in his book, which are reckoned past all credence." His *Il Milione* (*Description of the World*) is the most famous travel book ever written, yet even in Marco's own time there were people who doubted its authenticity.

Marco's alleged answer to the scoffers was that he had not told one half of what he had actually seen. That is precisely what has bothered some historians since—the things that are not in the book. Although it describes his apparent visit to China, there is no marveling at the Great Wall, no excitement at eating with chopsticks or drinking tea (which did not make it to Europe until the 17th century), no curiosity about the ritual binding of the feet of young girls.

Did Marco actually get to China and, if so, was his book a truthful account of his travels and his stay there? What sort of book was it? Was it a travel adventure, a merchant's handbook, or a guide for Christian missionaries? And was the story it told so groundbreaking, its impact on the age so powerful, as to justify its reputation as one of the great influences on European minds on the eve of the Age of Exploration?

Skepticism about Marco Polo has continued from the Middle Ages down to our own day. One of the reasons is that apart from the scant

Opposite: Marco Polo, with his father and his uncle, sets sail from Venice on the first stage of the three-year journey to the Far East and the court of the great Kublai Khan. They went by ship to Acre in Palestine and then overland to Hormuz on the Persian Gulf, through Persia, across Asia, and then into China. In the foreground the imaginative artist has tried to depict the lands that the Polos will visit and some of the strange things they will see.

"I believe it was God's will that we should come back, so men might know the things that are in the world." MARCO POLO, *IL MILIONE*, 1298

THE TRAVELS OF MARCO POLO

Polos return 1295

Polos depart 1271

EUROPE

ASIA

Venice

ITALY

Black Sea

Trabzon (Trebizond)

Caspian Sea

Polos reach Kashgar 1274

MONGOLIA

Polos arrive at Shangdu 1274

TURKEY

Tabriz (Tauris)

Balkh

Taloquan

Kashgar

Yumen

Shangdu "Xanadu"

Mediterranean Sea

Acre

IRAQ

IRAN (PERSIA)

AFGHANISTAN

CHINA

Beijing (Daidu)

Jerusalem

Persian Gulf

Minab (Hormuz)

PAKISTAN

Xian

Yangzhou

ARABIA

Junagadh

GUJARAT

INDIA

Hangzhou

AFRICA

Mumbai (Bombay)

ARABIAN SEA

MYANMAR (BURMA)

BAY OF BENGAL

Kunming

Quanzhou (Zaiton)

Polos leave China 1291

Thanjavur (Tanjore)

VIETNAM

KERALA

Kollam "Coilum"

Adam's Peak 7,360 ft 2,243 m

SRI LANKA (CEYLON)

ACEH

Belawan

INDIAN OCEAN

Sumatra

SINGAPORE

INDONESIA

— Route to China
— Route home
Historical names in parentheses
Modern political boundaries are shown.
Scale varies in this perspective.

biographical information given in his book, almost nothing else is known about him. From his book, we know he was born in 1254. His father was a Venetian merchant at a time when the commerce and trade of the maritime city states of Venice and Genoa was growing rapidly. The Venetian gold ducat, first minted in the 13th century, was on the way to becoming the standard European currency of the Middle Ages. And thanks to the Crusader conquest of Byzantium in the Crusade of 1204, Venice had gained possession of the port of Constantinople, at the crossroads between Europe and Asia.

By the mid-13th century many Venetian merchants had established themselves on the Black Sea, especially in the Crimean port of Soldaia. According to Marco's book it was from Soldaia that his father Niccolò and uncle Maffeo set out in around 1260 to trade in jewels, traveling eastward along the Silk Route through Central Asia. Things there had changed. Over the previous half-century the Mongols had conquered almost the whole of Asia. The Polo brothers were the first westerners to meet the great Kublai Khan, the new Mongol ruler of China. In 1269 they returned to Europe as ambassadors, carrying letters from Kublai to the pope.

Opposite: Marco Polo's will. In 1324, Marco died in Venice at the age of 70, leaving his wife and three daughters a substantial sum of money—though not the enormous fortune of which he had boasted. He also ordered that his Mongol servant Peter be set free.

MARCO POLO'S LAST WILL

Marco Polo		The Mongol Empire	
		1204	*The Fourth Christian Crusade to the Holy Land gains control of the port of Constantinople (Istanbul), opening up new trade opportunities with the East.*
		1215	*Beijing falls to the conquering Mongols, led by Genghis Khan.*
		1251	*The reign of Genghis's grandson Möngke marks the start of the "Mongol Peace." Trade across Mongol-controlled Central Asia flourishes.*
Marco Polo is born in the powerful republic of Venice.	1254		
		1258	*Mongol armies sack Baghdad, center of the Islamic world.*
Marco's father and uncle, Niccolò and Maffeo Polo, set out from Soldaia in search of new trade.	1260	1260	*Kublai Khan succeeds his brother Möngke as ruler of the vast Mongol Empire.*
Niccolò and Maffeo are invited to "Cathay" (China) to meet Kublai Khan.	1262	1266	*Kublai founds his new capital at Khanbaliq (Beijing / Peking).*
Marco Polo's travels begin.	1271		
The three Polos arrive in China, where Kublai Khan welcomes them.	1274	1279	*After defeating the Song dynasty, Kublai is recognized as the ruler of all China.*
Marco Polo escorts a Mongol princess to Hormuz on the Persian Gulf.	1292	1293	*The first Christian missionaries arrive in Beijing.*
Marco Polo returns to Venice.	1295	1294	*As Kublai Khan dies, the Mongol Empire stretches from modern-day Poland to Korea, split into four great khanates, or states. Soon after Kublai's death, the rulers of the Central Asian khanates convert to Islam.*
Marco is captured by the Genoese, who are at war with Venice. While in jail, he dictates the story of his travels.	1296		
Il Milione (Description of the World) is published.	1298		
Marco is freed and returns to Venice, where his stories are met with disbelief.	1299		
Marco Polo dies.	1324		
		1368	*The Mongols are driven out of China by Ming dynasty forces.*

> *"Many great and strange things in his book, which are reckoned past all credence."*

MARCO POLO'S BIOGRAPHER, JACOPO D'ACQUI, 1470S

Left: This manuscript illustration shows the vital Silk Route across Asia, linking Byzantium (modern Turkey) with China. It had been in operation for centuries before the Polos' time. Among other things, the Chinese traded their silk for medicines, perfumes, precious stones, ivory, and slaves from the West. Eventually, increased banditry led to a switch to seaborne trade and the route's consequent decline.

Two years later the brothers set out for China again, this time from Venice and accompanied by the young Marco, now aged 17. According to Marco's account, the journey to Kublai's court at his summer palace of Xanadu took three and a half years. The Polos spent the next 17 years in China, arriving back in Venice, after another three-year journey, in 1295. Imprisoned for a year or two in Genoa (for what offense remains unknown), Marco wrote his book with the help of a fellow inmate, a writer by the name of Rustichello da Pisa, who relied on Marco's memory, and notes and documents brought back from the East. In other words, he was a kind of ghostwriter. The book was finished in 1298.

Some modern historians have cast doubt on the story of the imprisonment and the way the book was supposed to have been written.

But whatever the story of its composition, the book gives a glowing picture of Marco. He is welcomed into Kublai's high counsels; he learns four languages (he does not say which); he is sent on important missions, one as far away as India. Yet, in all the official Chinese records of the time, no mention of these activities—or of his father and uncle—has ever been found.

Marco says that they delivered a letter from the pope and a phial of holy oil from the

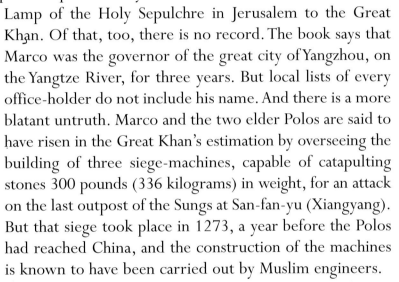

Lamp of the Holy Sepulchre in Jerusalem to the Great Khan. Of that, too, there is no record. The book says that Marco was the governor of the great city of Yangzhou, on the Yangtze River, for three years. But local lists of every office-holder do not include his name. And there is a more blatant untruth. Marco and the two elder Polos are said to have risen in the Great Khan's estimation by overseeing the building of three siege-machines, capable of catapulting stones 300 pounds (336 kilograms) in weight, for an attack on the last outpost of the Sungs at San-fan-yu (Xiangyang). But that siege took place in 1273, a year before the Polos had reached China, and the construction of the machines is known to have been carried out by Muslim engineers.

Above: Marco Polo's homeward journey from China took him along the western coast of India. This illustrator did his best to depict Indian vessels as Marco had described them, but they look more like European ships of the time, called cogs. Left: A contemporary illustration of a young Marco Polo.

But there is at least one mention of Marco in Chinese sources, in connection with the murder of a Saracen named Achmath. Renowned for his cruel tyranny, Achmath was beheaded with a sword by one Chenchu, or Wangchu. Marco tells the tale of this murder and his statement that "when all this happened Messer Marco was on the spot" is corroborated by a passage in Chinese annals. This reads, "The Emperor having returned from Chaghan-Nor to Shangru, desired Polo, Assessor of the Privy Council, to explain the reasons which had led Wangchu to commit this murder. Polo spoke with boldness of the crimes and oppressions of Achmath, which had rendered him an object of detestation throughout the Empire. The Emperor's eyes were opened, and he praised the courage of Wangchu."

For many of the more surprising omissions in Marco's account, reasonable explanations can be put forward. By the late 13th century, for instance, much of the Great Wall of China had crumbled. Most of what

"I have only told the half of what I saw."

MARCO POLO ON HIS DEATHBED, 1324

Below: Kublai Khan presents Marco's father and uncle with the golden tablet that served as their passport through the Mongol Empire. The letter they apparently carried from the khan to the pope asked for scholars to be sent to China to teach him about Christianity.

is visible today was built in the 15th and 16th centuries. Accounts of travels to China in the century after Marco's death in 1324 also fail to mention the Great Wall. In Marco's time the custom of drinking tea had established itself in south China, but in central and north China, where Marco spent most of his time, the habit was not yet widespread. Silences in *Il Milione* may raise suspicions, but they do not carry sufficient weight to demonstrate that the book was a hoax or intended as a deliberate fraud. As for what are clearly falsehoods, it may simply be that Marco wished to exaggerate the status that he achieved in China. And those falsehoods, as one historian has recently argued, "are of the sort which only someone who knew what he was talking about could have told."

Let us suppose that the book was a fraud written by someone, either Marco or another, who had never been to China. How then can the

wealth of detail about China and the Mongol Empire—material which historical research has now shown to be accurate—be explained? Some believe that the information was gathered from conversations with traders in the western reaches of the Mongol Empire—the land north and east of the Black Sea known as Tartary or the Khanate of the Golden Horde—or from contacts in Persia. As historians have pointed out, forms of language and place-names derived from Persian abound in the book, where one might expect words from the Mongol language.

To that specific objection it may be countered that Persian was the lingua franca (international language) used across the whole region and at the court of Kublai Khan at that time. It is possible to imagine the Polos wandering about western or central Asia for more than two decades, talking to travelers, listening to bazaar gossip, and amassing a vast amount of learning about the geography and customs of places that they had never visited. But is such a version of events really

likely? Other modern historians have pointed out what an unusual thing this would have been for them to do, without any visits by any of them back to Venice (to receive the Christian sacraments, for example) and also without their having been seen or recognized in any of these places by other western merchants, of whom there were increasing numbers by this time.

Historical controversy also surrounds the gold tablet, or *paiza*, which Marco says the Great Khan, Kublai, gave to his father and uncle and which passed into his possession. The tablet, an oblong sheet of gold with rounded corners, of about 12 by 3 inches (305 millimeters by 76 millimeters) in size, was worn around the neck. It was shown by the Polos on their journey back to Venice and on their return travels to China to guarantee them safe passage through the various provinces of the Mongol Empire. Some have suggested that a minor khan somewhere in the Mongol provinces gave the elder Polos the tablet. Maffeo, of course, may have been lying, but he said that the tablet came from "the magnificent Khan of the Tartars." Other historians believe such a grand phrase can only refer to the Great Khan Kublai.

The wealth of detail in Marco's book argues for its truthfulness. There is, for one thing, a long section containing descriptions of the physical characteristics of city after city in China—more than three dozen in total—and of the customs of their inhabitants. More tellingly, there is a section, though it is short and not very informative, on Japan (Marco calls it Zipangu) and on the Great Khan's abortive invasion of the island. Japan was otherwise unknown in central and western Asia or Europe until the 16th century. In other words, to have heard of Japan, Marco would have to have made it to China.

Above: Marco Polo attends a feast at the court of the Great Khan. Strangely enough, his book nowhere mentions that Chinese food is customarily eaten with chopsticks. The artist, who would never have seen a Mongolian, has depicted Kublai as European.

Above: An older, wiser, and bearded Marco Polo is depicted on this commemorative medallion. Fame was slow in coming for Marco—his Venetian contemporaries christened him the "man of a million lies" when they read of his adventures.

Il Milione portrays China as a society that is structured with a degree of order and efficiency unknown in the West. The cities are laid out in square grids with mathematical precision. The Great Khan is benevolent with his people, providing them with food in times of famine and hardship. In return, the people hold him in awe and, within miles of approaching his winter palace in Khanbahlu, fall silent as a mark of reverence. Rebellion is kept in check by armies stationed outside every city, armies whose personnel is changed every two years in order to stifle sedition in the ranks.

An elaborate postal system stretches out along the roads from the capital to the provinces, with large posting-houses. Each posting-house has 400 horses to carry the royal messengers, and over the empire as a whole there are 200,000 such horses. Paper currency, printed at the mint in Khanbahlu, is used in the capital and in many other cities—"nor dares any person, at the peril of his life, refuse to accept it in payment." Then there is "a sort of black stone" that is dug out of the mountains, "where it runs in veins;" when lit, it "burns like charcoal and retains the fire much better than wood." Thanks to coal (Marco does not use the word), every man of rank or wealth could enjoy a warm bath two or three times a week.

The dominant impression left by Marco's account, which has almost nothing to say of the poverty of the Chinese peasantry, is of a land teeming with wealth far surpassing anything known in the West. The forecourt alone of the Great Khan's winter palace at Khanbahlu, "the most extensive that has ever yet been known," is a square measuring 8 miles (13km) along each side. For bodyguards, the emperor has 12,000 horsemen. For his birthday celebrations, he clothes 20,000 nobles and military officers in gold silk. They bring presents to him and according to the custom "furnish nine times nine of the article of which the present consists." So, if a province sends a present of horses, it sends 81. For his birthday the Great Khan receives no fewer than 100,000 horses.

Accompanying him on his hunting trip to the north, after wintering in Khanbahlu, are leopards and lynxes to chase deer; lions larger than Babylonian lions to seize boars, oxen, deer, and other beasts; and eagles to catch wolves. There are also 10,000 falconers. This hunt, which lasts for the months of March, April, and May, "is unrivaled by any other

amusement in the world." Perhaps the Great Khan saw things a bit differently—he had four wives and hundreds of concubines.

Il Milione is not an adventure book, nor what is nowadays thought of as a travel book. It does not recount dangers and hazards overcome, nor record conversations with strangers along the way. Nor is it a handbook for merchants. Although it provided the first comprehensive catalog of spices and where they were to be found, it did not offer Venetian readers much insight into how to do business in the East. Its real points of focus are geography and Mongol culture.

Marco's prose is humdrum. The long list of cities may be tedious. But his book gave medieval readers their first glimpse of a new world, a populous world filled with large cities, a world of great prosperity and bustling commerce—a world, in short, far richer than anything in Europe, and richer than anything previously imagined by Europeans. Christopher Columbus himself read it carefully, making special note of the rare and precious gemstones mentioned in it. Whether Marco Polo did or did not reach China, it was his book that played a major part in inspiring the urge to find a sea route to the lands that he described.

Above: Kublai Khan himself presides over the execution of a convicted criminal while officials of his court look on. Mongol justice was swift and sure—the khan was described by Marco as a benevolent dictator whose decisions were not to be questioned.

WHO BUILT GREAT ZIMBABWE AND WHY?

In the 1500s, Portuguese merchants were the first Europeans to hear tales of a vast complex of stone buildings that rose out of nowhere in deepest Africa. In 1867, the truth of the rumors was confirmed when Adam Renders, an American-born German hunter and explorer, accidentally stumbled across the actual remains. Now the questions began in earnest. Who built what came to be known as Great Zimbabwe? Who lived there? What led to the settlement's decline and abandonment? Modern archaeology has provided answers to some of these questions, but, even today, there are mysteries to be solved.

Above: King Solomon welcomes the Queen of Sheba. Based on what they had heard about the Great Zimbabwe ruins, it was early Portuguese traders on the east African coast who came up with the (mistaken) notion that the site had been the queen's capital.

The site occupies nearly 1,800 acres (730 hectares), divided into three distinct areas—the Hill Complex, the Great Enclosure, and the Valley Complex—all built of granite from a nearby quarry. The Hill Complex, which resembles a fort but was not, stands imposingly on a summit above the valley and consists of a number of stone enclosures. The most impressive feature is the elliptical Great Enclosure, which stretches over 800 feet (245 meters). Its outer walls, decorated with a distinctive chevron pattern, were 32 feet (9.7 meters) high and in some places as much as 17 feet (5 meters) thick. Smaller walls formed a series of enclosures in the Valley Complex. What has always struck observers is how tightly fitting, without mortar (rather like the castle walls of medieval Europe), the granite slabs are. At its peak, the city, for that is what it was, appears to have been inhabited by as many as 20,000 people. The elite lived within the walled enclosures, the rest in clay-and-gravel huts huddled outside.

Archaeologists and historians alike have struggled to explain the existence of so imposing a city. Based on what he had heard, João de Barros, a Portuguese historian writing in 1552, thought that it was Axum, one of the cities of the biblical Queen of Sheba. Others, linking its existence to the region's gold trade, held that it must be Ophir, from

"The names of King Solomon and the Queen of Sheba were on everybody's lips."

THEODORE BENT, COMMISSIONED TO INVESTIGATE THE ORIGINS OF GREAT ZIMBABWE BY CECIL RHODES, 1893

where the queen obtained gold for the Temple of Solomon. The notion of a link with Sheba persisted. Carl Mauch, a German explorer who visited the site in 1871, thought that the Great Enclosure, which he said the local people called *mumbahru* (house of the great woman), was built for the queen.

What 19th-century Europeans found impossible to credit was that Africans themselves could have been responsible for Great Zimbabwe's

Above: More stone was used in the building of the Great Enclosure's outer wall than in the rest of the complexes put together.

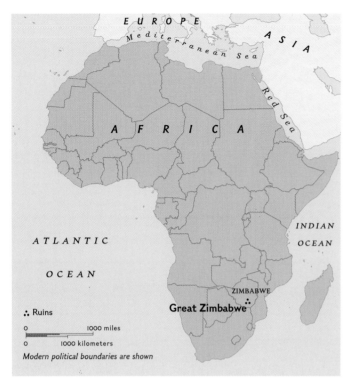

Ruins

0   1000 miles

0   1000 kilometers

Modern political boundaries are shown

creation. Shockingly, Adam Renders told Mauch that so large a city "could never have been built by blacks." When he visited the site in the 1890s, Cecil Rhodes (1853–1902), the architect of British imperialism in southern Africa, told the local Bantu chiefs that he had come to see "the ancient temple that once upon a time belonged to white men." Theodore Bent, hired by Rhodes to investigate the origins of the complex, continued to believe this, even though the evidence was staring him in the face. He found a host of remains, such as pottery relics; bronze and copper spearheads, adzes and axes; and tools for working gold. These were similar to objects used by the Bantu themselves. He concluded that the complex had been built by "a northern race coming from Arabia... closely akin to the Phoenician and Egyptian."

It was thanks to the work of the archaeologist David Randall-MacIver that the true origins of Great Zimbabwe finally began to emerge. In 1906, he announced that the mud dwellings on the site were "unquestionably African in every detail" and belonged to a period "which is fixed by foreign imports as, in general, medieval." Support came from Gertrude Caton-Thompson, a contemporary archaeologist, who identified Chinese and Persian artifacts found on the site as imports dating from the 1300s to the 1500s. She also found a number of objects that had clearly been produced locally. Caton-Thompson excavated the site down to its bedrock, and in every stratigraphic layer she discovered remains of an African way of life. Great Zimbabwe was not an ancient city. Nor did it yield up any evidence of having been built and inhabited by white men.

Radiocarbon dating carried out in the 1960s showed that the Hill Complex was built around 1250, the buildings inside the Great Enclosure sometime in the 1300s, and the great exterior walls, together with the Valley Complex, somewhat later. As to who built it, there is no completely definite answer. The accepted view now is that it was built

Opposite (top): An engraving of the 33-foot-high (10 meters) Conical Tower in the Great Enclosure. The enclosure itself could have been a royal court, a religious center, or perhaps a place of initiation for young men approaching adulthood. Opposite (below): A close-up of the brickwork reveals just how sophisticated the building methods of the creators of Great Zimbabwe must have been to ensure the stones held together without mortar. The ruins of Great Zimbabwe are without doubt the most impressive archaeological site in sub-Saharan Africa.

Great Zimbabwe			Africa
The first stone building begins among the Iron Age peoples living on the central plateau region of modern-day Zimbabwe. The population lives in small village communities, ruled over by dynasties of chiefs, called Karanga.	c.1000		
		1040	*The fundamentalist Muslim Berber Almoravids invade Morocco.*
		c.1050	*The Islamic Swahili city states along the east coast of Africa exploit trading links across the Indian Ocean and with inland states.*
Gold- and copper-mining begins. The trade in gold with Arab merchants along the coast of present-day Mozambique is controlled by the Karanga. Wealth steadily increases.	c.1200		
		1240	*The Islamic empire of Mali is founded. Mali goes on to control the trans-Saharan trade in slaves and gold.*
The Hill Complex at Great Zimbabwe is built as a centre for trade and cattle-rearing.	c.1250		
		c.1270	*The Christian kingdom of Ethiopia enters a period of expansion.*
The Great Enclosure at Great Zimbabwe is built. At its height, the city is home to 20,000 people and maintains a standing army.	c.1300	c.1340	*The Great Mosque of Jenne is built in Mali.*
		1427	*Envoys from the Ethiopian emperor reach Spain, asking for an alliance against the Muslim world.*
		1441	*The first African slaves are shipped to Portugal. An Act of Union is signed between the Church of Ethiopia and the Church of Rome.*
The kingdom of Great Zimbabwe falls into decline, probably for economic and political reasons.	c.1450	c.1450	*An Islamic university is founded at Timbuktu in west Africa.*
		c.1465	*The empire of Songhay becomes the leading power in west Africa.*
		1470	*The Portuguese start attacking the Gold Coast of west Africa.*
Great Zimbabwe is already abandoned.	1500	1500	*The Portuguese set up trading posts along the east African coast.*
		1502	*The first African slaves are shipped to the New World.*
Tales of fantastic wealth make their way to the coast via Swahili traders. Portuguese explorer Antonio Fernandes enters the area. He is just the first of many traders and missionaries.	1513		

> *"A square fortress, masonry without and within, built of stones of marvelous size, and there appears to be no mortar joining them."*

HISTORIAN JOÃO DE BARROS, *DA ASIA*, 1552

Above: Taken from inside the Great Enclosure, this photo shows the Hill Complex in the background. Great Zimbabwe stands in the midst of wooded savanna backed by bare granite hills, which would have provided the stone that was needed for its building.

by the Shona, the ancestors of the present-day Bantu—the very name "Zimbabwe" is generally thought to be a contraction of the Shona phrase "*dzimba dza mabwe*" (houses of stone).

Why Great Zimbabwe was built is no easier a question to answer. It was once thought that its founding was sparked off by the presence of a rich gold mine. Most of the gold found there, however, came from the upper levels of the archaeological deposits, which suggests that locally mined gold was of significance only well after the founding. Even so, gold may hold the clue to a possible solution. For over 200 years, Great Zimbabwe was an important hub on the trading route between the gold-producing regions farther south and the ports on the coast of Mozambique where African gold and ivory were exchanged for goods from Arabia and the Far East. It also was able to supply objects made of tin, copper, and iron to the coastal settlements. It is probable that its ruler was powerful enough to demand tribute—or taxes paid in goods—from lesser chiefs in the region. The Great Enclosure, which early investigators thought might have been used for gold smelting, is now believed to have served as a royal residence, perhaps exclusively for the ruler's wife.

The ruler himself was a semi-divine figure, and Great Zimbabwe almost certainly functioned as a religious center. In fact, the Great Enclosure is often referred to as a temple. It holds a number of towers. One of them—the Conical Tower—is notable for its large beehive-shape. It is solid and appears to have served no practical purpose. It is possible it was intended to represent a grain elevator, symbolizing—and aiming to attract—good harvests and prosperity. Praying to the gods for rain and abundant crops is an ancient Shona tradition and there is evidence that Great Zimbabwe remained a place for the practice of such rituals long after it was largely deserted in the late 1400s.

Another theory suggests that the Hill Complex, rather than the Great Enclosure, was the spiritual center of the complex. It contained what appear to have been altars and at least 30 granite and soapstone statues. Placed on the tops of columns, the statues may have represented the spirits of former rulers and been part of a tradition of ancestor worship. Their concentration is a strong indication that they had a central role to play in some kind of religious ceremony.

By 1500, Great Zimbabwe was abandoned. Once again, historians can make only educated guesses at the reasons. The poor soil of the savanna around the site would not have sustained agriculture on the scale required to feed the city's population. It may be, therefore, that local sources of food dwindled, so sparking off the abandonment. Another factor was undoubtedly a shift in trading patterns to the north and the rise of the neighboring states of Torwa and Mutapa.

Whatever the causes of Great Zimbabwe's decline, it remains one of the most fascinating lost civilizations of the world. Its spectacular ruins are a potent testament to the fact that, contrary to long-accepted European beliefs, early Africa was by no means the "Dark Continent" of myth and legend.

Above: British-born empire-builder and tycoon Cecil Rhodes was not universally popular, as this French cartoon confirms—it shows him standing on a landscape of dead bodies. The investigation Rhodes sponsored into the origins of Great Zimbabwe confirmed the blinkered European view that it was of non-African origin, largely by ignoring the evidence of the artifacts that were uncovered.

DID THE CHINESE BEAT CHRISTOPHER COLUMBUS TO THE NEW WORLD?

For hundreds of years, most Westerners believed that the Italian Christopher Columbus was the first explorer to reach the New World, when the three ships of his tiny fleet made their landfall in the Caribbean in 1492. However, in 1957 came the discovery of the so-called Vinland map, which seemed to support the theory that the Vikings had beaten Columbus by nearly 500 years. Then, just as the authenticity of the map was being scientifically challenged, a new, unexpected contender arrived. The medieval Chinese are now emerging as candidates to topple the great Italian from his pedestal.

Above: A 17th-century print shows the explorer Zheng He seated under an awning on board his flagship. Among the animals he brought back to the imperial court from his great voyages were what the Chinese called "camel birds" and "celestial horses" (ostriches and zebras).

The story starts in 1402, when Zhu Di, the fourth son of the first emperor of the Ming dynasty, succeeded to the Chinese throne. In his quest for power he had been faithfully served by an official called Zheng He, who took the title of Grand Eunuch. Within a year, Zheng He was appointed commander-in-chief of the Chinese navy.

Already, during the Tang dynasty (618–907), China had begun to build ocean-going ships, and the early Ming Empire possessed one of the largest fleets the world had yet seen. (The Venetian fleet, the next most powerful in the world, consisted of about 300 small galleys, suitable only for Mediterranean voyages.) But even this was not large enough for the ambitious emperor's purposes. One of Zhu Di's first acts was to commission the building of 1,681 new ships, including many so-called "treasure ships." These were huge square-rigged junks with nine masts. They also had enormous holds for carrying trading goods to and from China. Their rudders alone measured 36 feet (11 meters)—almost as long as the *Santa Clara*, one of the caravels in

Opposite: The massive walls of Beijing's Forbidden City were so-called because ordinary Chinese people were banned from entering it. Emperor Zhu Di ordered the city to be built to house him and his court. It took 14 years and an estimated 200,000 men to complete it.

"A pivotal moment in the history of man's knowledge of the globe."

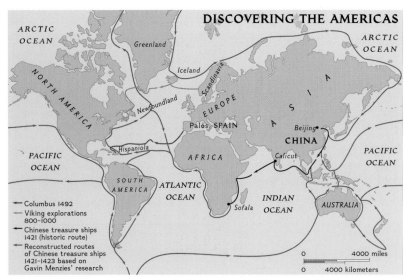

DISCOVERING THE AMERICAS

ARCTIC OCEAN

Greenland

Iceland

ARCTIC OCEAN

NORTH AMERICA

Newfoundland

Scandinavia

EUROPE

ASIA

Palos, SPAIN

Beijing

CHINA

PACIFIC OCEAN

Hispaniola

AFRICA

Calicut

PACIFIC OCEAN

SOUTH AMERICA

ATLANTIC OCEAN

Sofala

INDIAN OCEAN

AUSTRALIA

← Columbus 1492
← Viking explorations 800–1000
← Chinese treasure ships 1421 (historic route)
← Reconstructed routes of Chinese treasure ships 1421–1423 based on Gavin Menzies' research

0   4000 miles
0   4000 kilometers

which Columbus and his men were to cross the Atlantic. Zhu Di's fleet now totaled 3,500 vessels, about 250 of which were gigantic treasure ships.

Zhu Di's ambition was to send forth his fleet to discover the whole of the world, to map it, and, perhaps, to bring more and more foreign rulers within China's tribute system. This was the system by which outsiders paid symbolical tribute to China, usually by donating specimens of produce or animals typical of their country. In return they received special trading rights with China and Chinese protection against their enemies. The enterprise was not simply commercial in concept. While Europe was an economic backwater still emerging from the Dark Ages, China was unsurpassed anywhere in the world in its learning and technology. It already had gunpowder, printing, and paper currency. Beijing was the richest city on earth. Zhu Di commissioned more than 2,000 scholars to compile an encyclopedia with 4,000 volumes. (In comparison, during the same period of history, the library of King Henry V of England contained only six handwritten books.) The encyclopedia was completed in 1421, although most of the volumes were never printed. In keeping with this spirit of intellectual enquiry, Zhu Di expected his overseas explorers to bring back information about the geography, history, customs, and commerce of lands and peoples from around the world.

Zhu Di had moved the Ming capital from Nanjing to Beijing in 1404. There he constructed the Forbidden City, a monumental walled complex of richly decorated palaces, temples, and other buildings. The splendor of the ceremonies which attended its inauguration were evidence of China's unrivaled wealth and of the emperor's resolve to display it to the world. On February 2, 1421, the beginning of the Chinese New Year, 28 foreign rulers and ambassadors converged on Beijing for the grand opening of the Forbidden City. The potentates were lavishly entertained for an entire month, their departure coinciding

Opposite: A statue of the Viking explorer Leif Ericsson (970–1020), who, according to some, discovered America long before Columbus. The medieval Vinland map, purporting to show early Viking knowledge of the Americas, is now being labeled a clever 20th-century forgery. This means there is no hard historical evidence to confirm that Ericsson made the discovery. If he did, his most likely landfall was either New England or Newfoundland.

China		The World	
The Ming dynasty is founded as the Mongols are driven from China.	1368		
		1369	*Hostilities are renewed in the Hundred Years' War between England and France.*
		1400	*Londoner Geoffrey Chaucer dies, leaving unfinished his groundbreaking masterpiece,* The Canterbury Tales.
Zhu Di comes to the Chinese throne.	1402		
Zhu Di decides to move the capital to Beijing, and starts to build the Forbidden City.	1404		*At around this time, leprosy dies out in Europe.*
Admiral Zheng He starts his voyages of discovery.	1405		
		1408	*In Florence, Donatello sculpts* David, *an early milestone of Renaissance art.*
Zheng He sets out on his sixth maritime expedition. At home, steps are taken to restore civil order: lower taxation, reorganization of the bureaucracy, and the establishment of the secret service.	1421	1421	*The Portuguese, the first great European explorers, take their initial steps abroad by setting up a colony on Madeira, an island off the coast of north Africa.*
The last ships of the 1421 expedition return home, perhaps after having "discovered" the New World.	1423	1423	*In Italy, the 30-year war between Milan and Florence begins.*
Zhu Di dies, and China starts to turn inward.	1424		
The construction of ocean-going junks is banned.	1433		
		1434	*Filippo Brunelleschi completes his feat of Renaissance engineering: the great dome of Florence cathedral.*
One of many peasant rebellions takes place across China.	1440	1440	*Montecuhzoma I becomes ruler of the Aztecs in Mexico.*
Ming porcelain production is at its peak, with the building of a new factory. Porcelain is exported to east Africa by Arab traders, from where Portuguese merchants take it to Europe.	1460	1460	*In England, Richard, Duke of York, is killed during the Wars of the Roses, between the houses of York and Lancaster.*
		1487	*Portuguese explorer Bartolomeu Dias rounds the Cape of Good Hope of southern Africa, the first European to do so.*
The 1,700-year-old Great Wall is restored, to aid defense.	1488		
		1492	*Christopher Columbus "discovers" the New World when he lands on the Bahamas while searching for a new sea route to the Far East.*

"I should steer southwest to go there... in the spheres which I have seen and in the drawings of mappae mundi it is in this region."

CHRISTOPHER COLUMBUS IN HIS LOG BOOK ON THE HUNT FOR THE NEW WORLD, REVEALING THAT HE KNEW HE WAS NOT THE FIRST TO REACH IT, OCTOBER 24, 1492

with the launch of the latest and greatest of the emperor's ambitious ocean-going enterprises.

The Chinese had a wealth of seafaring experience. The great armada of four fleets—with about 30 ships in each—that set sail across the Yellow Sea on March 5, 1421 was their sixth great maritime expedition since 1405. Chinese astronomers had been charting the positions of the night stars for 2,000 years, and mariners understood how to use the Pole Star and magnetic compasses to calculate their position. Previous expeditions sponsored by Zhu Di had traveled beyond southeastern Asia, reaching the Persian Gulf and the east coast of Africa.

The Chinese junks could remain on the high seas for three months at a time, covering 4,500 miles (7,200 kilometers) before having to make landfall. Their sheer bulk and ingenious construction (divided into separate compartments, each of which was sealed by watertight bulkheads) minimized the dangers from typhoons, ice floes, and reefs. The treasure ships were accompanied by grain-carriers and water-tankers. Citrus fruit was taken on board to prevent scurvy, and brown rice to stave off beri-beri.

The voyages that set out that March were to take the Chinese thousands of miles. Six weeks after leaving home, they arrived at the Malaysian port of Malacca, virtually a colony of China and, lying halfway between China and India, the center of trading activity in southeastern Asia and the Indian Ocean. Zheng He himself then returned home. The fleets themselves sailed on to

Left: Christopher Columbus (1451–1506) was a Genoese navigator and explorer. He convinced the rulers of Spain, Ferdinand and Isabella, that, by sailing west, he could find a new sea route to the riches of the East. Below: In 1492, Columbus and his men take their first steps on to the shores of what was to prove to be the New World.

Calicut, in southern India, then to Sofala, in modern Mozambique, returning the foreign dignitaries to their homelands along the way.

This is as far as confirmed history stretches, since the account of the expedition in the diaries of a contemporary Chinese historian, Ma Huan, ends here. What historian Gavin Menzies argues, though, is that the Chinese sailed on and on. Swept onward by the Aghulas current that flows southward along the east coast of Africa, their ships rounded the Cape of Good Hope by about the beginning of August, 1421, three weeks after leaving Sofala. Two months later, the trade winds had blown them to central west Africa, where a landfall was made at a place labeled as "Garbin" on contemporary maps. From there, the south equatorial current took them round the bulge of Africa to the Cape Verde Islands. Less than a month later they sighted the coast of Brazil. From there the fleets proceeded south, rounding the tip of South America via what we now know as the Strait of Magellan.

From the tip of South America, says Menzies, one fleet headed south to the Falklands Islands, the South Shetlands, and on to Graham Land, in the northern reaches of Antarctica, in search of a southern equivalent of the Pole Star by which to determine latitude. And the Chinese found it—the Crucis Alpha, the leading star of the Southern Cross. A sailors' manual compiled in 1433, entitled the *Wu Pei Chi*, confirms that by that time the Chinese had learned how to determine southern latitudes. By the end of the expedition, too, the likelihood is that the fleets must have discovered a way of calculating longitude, though precisely what method they used to do so remains an unknown.

From Antarctica, some ships apparently ventured up the west coast of South America and on to California. Others returned to China by an eastward route, visiting Australasia along the way. Meanwhile, one of the fleets had made its way from the Cape Verde Islands to the Caribbean and the eastern shores of what we now call the United States and Canada, finally visiting Greenland and Iceland before heading home via the Arctic Ocean. After two and a half years at sea, the last ships finally

Above: This map of the world dates from 1490. It is an accurate reflection of what European mapmakers knew about the world at the time, based upon the discoveries made by the early explorers.

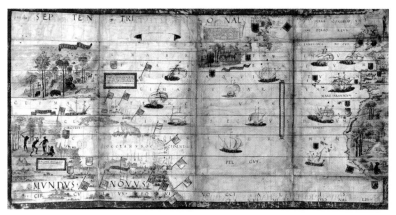

Above: An early 16th-century Portuguese map of the Atlantic Ocean, showing the Old World and the New World. Portuguese holdings in the latter were limited to Brazil. The Spanish had the rest.

limped into their home port in the fall of 1423. A century before Magellan, the Chinese had sailed round the world.

What makes all this plausible is the sheer weight of evidence that Menzies draws on to support his argument. He refers to maps, stone carvings, artifacts, flora and fauna, remains of shipwrecks, and DNA analysis. The so-called Ryukoku map, for instance, drawn in Korea and originally dating from 1403 but modified after 1420, charts the west coast of Africa so accurately that it almost certainly must have been made by someone who had sailed around the Cape. The sole remaining fragment of the Chinese Mao Kun map, compiled after the expedition, shows the Chinese armada at the southern tip of Africa.

Some early maps made by Europeans are equally puzzling—more because of what they include than what they leave out. By definition, these maps date from long before the great Portuguese and Spanish voyages of discovery started, yet they still show remarkable geographic details that historically were thought not to have been discovered until those selfsame voyages took place. Though none of the maps indicates that the places charted on them were visited by the Chinese, their accuracy leaves no doubt that someone did, and China alone had the economic, scientific, and naval strength to have done so.

If this argument is accepted, the question is how this information got from China to Europe. Someone, it seems, must have brought back copies of maps showing the discoveries made by the Chinese. If so, it is likely that Arab sea traders were responsible. These traders regularly plied the seas between the Arab world and southern China, mainly in order to supply Venice with spices, and the Asians with African and European goods. It could well have been these traders who made use of, and passed on, the Chinese knowledge.

Yet Zhu Di did not reap the benefit of his discoveries. The costs of building the Forbidden City and expanding the fleet placed a terrible burden on the Chinese economy. Grain shortages provoked revolts, and rebellions spread through the empire. When Zhu Di died in 1424, the new emperor and

Below: This European engraving shows various types of Chinese boats, though somewhat surprisingly no giant junks are seen. This may be because the engraving was made after Zhu Di's successor had ordered the scrapping of the Chinese ocean-going fleet.

his advisors decided it was time to call a halt. A series of edicts banned overseas trade and travel. Shipbuilding ceased, and the records of Zheng He's voyages were deliberately destroyed. China turned inward.

As far as the question of who got to America first is concerned, the jury is still out. The apparently 15th-century Vinland map shows the northeast coast of America, with next to it the Latin legend "Island of Vinland, discovered by Bjarni and Leif in company." If genuine, it is the oldest map of America, and commemorates the Viking explorer Leif Ericsson's journey to the area in the 10th century. The parchment on which the map is drawn is unquestionably medieval, earlier than Columbus's voyage of 1492, as radiocarbon dating in 2002 has proved.

The real controversy is about the age of the ink used to draw the map. Some experts say that the most recent chemical analysis shows for certain that some of the ink contains traces of a chemical compound unknown before the 1920s. This, they argue, finally proves that the map is a clever fake. Kirsten Seaver, a California-based Norwegian historian, has even come up with the name of the possible forger—Joseph Fischer, a German Jesuit priest and medieval scholar. Seaver believes Fischer's motive for faking the map in the 1930s was possibly in protest against Nazi exploitation of ancient Norse history for propaganda. Others point out that traces of the selfsame compound have been found in other undoubtedly medieval documents and that the amounts involved are so small that their presence could be coincidental. Though radiocarbon dating the ink might settle things, the current technology will not work with the limited amount of ink actually on the map.

As for the Chinese, the evidence that they got to America first, though impressive, is circumstantial. It could turn out that it was Columbus after all. What is undisputed is that the continent had been peopled long before any of this took place: the first people living in North America were undoubtedly the prehistoric nomads who either crossed the land bridge that once linked the north of the continent and Asia or arrived by sea toward the end of the great Ice Age.

Below: This late 16th-century Chinese map of the world incorporates information brought to China by Jesuit missionaries from Europe. By this time, the wheel had turned full circle. China had turned in on itself, abandoning Zhu Di's policy of aggressive exploration of the outside world.

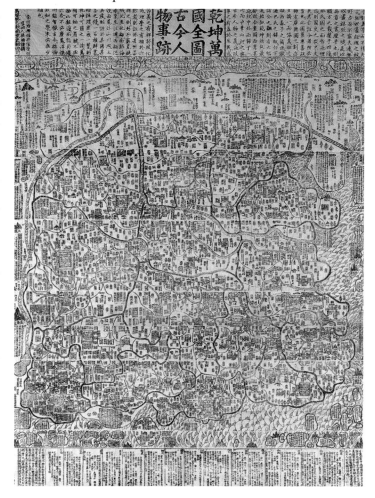

WHAT IS THE TRUTH BEHIND THE LEGEND OF EL DORADO?

Old maps of Brazil and Guyana in South America sometimes show a place called El Dorado, but its location is never precisely marked. This is for a good reason, because this legendary city of gold, which fired the imagination of European treasure-hunters for centuries, has never been found. Recently, however, modern archaeological investigators have come up with a new theory of what El Dorado really was, which does not involve gold at all.

Humanity's obsession with gold dates from time immemorial. And the Spanish soldier-explorers of the New World were as obsessed as any other people at any other time in history. It was the lure of gold that tempted the mighty Greek leader Alexander the Great to march on Persia, seduced the Portuguese into sailing off the map and breaking the bounds of the medieval world, and brought Columbus across the Atlantic to the Americas. Now it inspired a search that was to last for centuries, cost thousands of lives, and, even today, remains unresolved. It was the quest for the riches of El Dorado, the so-called "gilded man," and for Manoa, his city of gold—both known simply as El Dorado in the popular imagination.

It was in the western regions of the vast stretch of land lying between the Amazon and Orinoco Rivers on the South American mainland that the Spanish first heard a version of the legend in the mid-1530s. The local Muisca Indians told them of the mystic rituals of a sun-worshipping tribe called the Chibcha, who venerated gold as the favored metal of their god. They wore golden ornaments and for centuries had covered their buildings with sheets of precious metal. Even more interesting from the Spanish standpoint, was the part gold was reported to play in one aspect of the Chibchas' religious beliefs.

Once a year or perhaps more often, so the tale ran, the servants of the tribe's chief, or king, would smear him with sticky resin and blow

Left: A gold mask made by the Incas in Peru. One version of the El Dorado legend was that the fabled city was founded by a band of Incas, fleeing with their treasures in the face of Spanish invasion in the 1530s. Opposite: This drawing of Manoa is from a 1599 account of Sir Walter Raleigh's search for El Dorado. Raleigh believed the city was located on an island in a lake he called Parime, in Guyana.

*"He went about all covered with powdered gold,
as casually as if it were powdered salt."*

GONZALO FERNÁNDEZ DE OVIEDO, *HISTORY OF THE INDIES*, 1535

gold dust over him until he glistened in gold from head to foot. Then he was led in procession to a raft, which was towed to the middle of a sacred lake. Plunging into the icy water, the chief rinsed the gold dust off his body while the others cast priceless offerings of gold and precious stones into the waters.

The Muisca told the Spanish that the lake in question was Lake Guatavita, lying in the hills about 31 miles (50km) northeast of

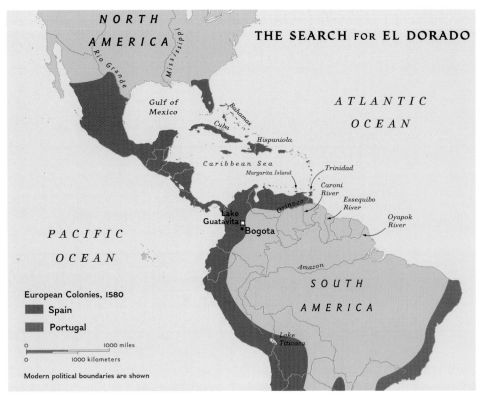

NORTH AMERICA

Rio Grande

Mississippi

Gulf of Mexico

Bahamas

Cuba

Hispaniola

Caribbean Sea

Margarita Island

Trinidad

Caroni River

Essequibo River

Orinoco

Oyapok River

Lake Guatavita

Bogota

Amazon

SOUTH AMERICA

ATLANTIC OCEAN

PACIFIC OCEAN

THE SEARCH FOR EL DORADO

Lake Titicaca

European Colonies, 1580

■ Spain

■ Portugal

0   1000 miles
0   1000 kilometers

Modern political boundaries are shown

Opposite: Two gold ornaments from Colombia, dating from before the Spanish conquest. The top one represents a shaman, or wise man. The bottom one is a seated figure, maybe that of a tribal chief, and is from the 14th or 15th century.

present-day Bogotá in Colombia, so it was there that they began their search for the treasures they were convinced lay buried at the lake's bottom. A first attempt found nothing. Another, organized by a Bogotá merchant called Antonio de Sepulveda in the 1580s, was a little more successful. He employed thousands of Indians to cut a large wedge out of the rim of the lake in order to drain it. The result was disaster—at least for the Indians. When the water level had fallen by about 60 feet (18 meters), the walls of the wedge caved in, killing many of the workers. But some treasure was found. It included a gold breastplate, a staff covered with gold plaques, and an emerald the size of a chicken's egg. These were sent as gifts to King Philip II of Spain.

This was by no means the El Dorado the Spanish were looking for—indeed by this time the main thrust of the search had already switched eastward. This was hardly surprising, for wherever the conquistadors (as the Spanish explorers are known to history) went, they heard differing tales and rumors about the location of the city they were seeking. This, so they were constantly being assured, lay only a few days' march farther away. The Colombian mountains had proved practically impassable, with every expedition there either running out of food or being decimated and forced to retreat in the face of hostile Indians. Surely, the Spanish reasoned, they would have better luck elsewhere, in the unexplored jungles of the Amazon basin. Sadly for them, this, too, proved not to be the case. As new regions were explored, the location of El Dorado shifted and shifted. It was always across the next ridge or deeper in the jungle. Descriptions of it became more and more elaborate as well—even the cooking pots and the trees were said to be made of precious gold.

Probably the most determined effort the Spanish made to find the fabled city was led by Antonio de Berrío, the governor of Guyana and

New World		Old World	
Christopher Columbus, sponsored by Spain, "discovers" the New World when he lands on the Bahamas.	1492	1492	Granada, the last Muslim kingdom in Spain, falls to Ferdinand and Isabella of Spain. All Jews are expelled from the country by royal edict.
Columbus sets up the first Spanish settlement in the New World, on Hispaniola (modern Santo Domingo).	1496		
John Cabot, sponsored by the English, "discovers" Newfoundland.	1497	1497	Norway, Sweden, and Denmark are united under King John of Denmark.
Pedro Álvares Cabral claims Brazil for Portugal.	1500	c.1500	Inuit peoples have settled the whole Arctic region.
The first African slaves arrive in the Caribbean.	1502	1502	German locksmith Peter Henlein invents the pocket watch.
The cartographer Waldseemüller's map names America after the Italian explorer Amerigo Vespucci, whom he mistakenly thought had discovered the New World.	1507		
		1508	Michelangelo begins the ceiling of the Sistine Chapel in Rome.
The Spanish start to settle Central America.	1509	1509	The Ethiopians send an ambassador to Portugal.
Florida is claimed by Spain.	1513		
All natives of the New World are forced to convert to Christianity.	1514	1514	The Pole Nicolaus Copernicus proposes that the earth revolves around the sun.
The Spanish force the Aztecs to surrender their capital, Tenochtitlán. Mexico City is founded on the ruins.	1521	1521	Martin Luther, founder of Protestantism, is excommunicated from the Roman Catholic Church.
The Incas are conquered by Spanish forces.	1533	1533	Henry VIII of England marries Anne Boleyn, although the pope has refused to annul his previous marriage. Henry is excommunicated, leading to a total break with the Church of Rome.
The Spanish conquer the Mayans.	1545		
Jesuit missionaries in Brazil urge humane treatment of the Indian population.	1551	1556	Akbar inherits the Indian Moghal Empire. He embarks on a campaign to integrate Muslims and Hindus in his realm, and to expand his domains.
Most of the Indians in Brazil are wiped out by war and disease.	c.1562		
After massacring the French settlers, the Spanish set up the first permanent settlement in North America, at St. Augustine in Florida.	1565	1580	Philip of Spain takes the Portuguese crown, and becomes king of all the two countries' lands in the New World.

Above (top): The Spanish meet the Aztecs in the 16th century. Above (bottom): Spanish conquistadors with their native Tlazcalan allies attack an Aztec temple. Mexico had its own El Dorado—the legendary Seven Cities of Gold. But nothing was ever found.

Trinidad, who arrived there in 1580 at the age of 60. Berrío had a particular interest in the quest. His wife was a niece of Gonzalo Jiménez de Quesada, who had himself looked for the golden city, while at the same time amassing a fortune by stealing treasure from the Indian tribes. He had also set up and run an extremely profitable emerald mine. On his death, Quesada willed his estates to his niece and hence they came to Berrío. A clause in the will specifically required him to continue the search.

Berrío had come to the view that El Dorado had to be situated behind the mountains of Guyana—an idea that was given further credence by the supposed stories of Juan Martínez, a Spanish survivor of an earlier expedition. Martínez, after being taken prisoner and living for years among the Indians, turned up on the Spanish-held island of Margarita at the mouth of the Orinoco in about 1586. He claimed, so it is said, that, during his captivity, he was blindfolded and led on a four-day march to an unknown destination. When the blindfold was removed, he found himself gazing upon a city whose houses were made of gold and precious stones. He was taken to the palace of the king—El Dorado—who, he learned, was bathed in gold dust and anointed with fragrant spices and herbs every day. Martínez went on to locate the city, which he said the king called Manoa, on the banks of Lake Parima in the Rupununi district. Modern writers, however, doubt that Martínez ever existed.

By this time, Berrío had already launched two expeditions, in 1584 and 1585, with a third following in 1591. The last expedition, undertaken by a band of about 120 men, followed the Orinoco into the highlands in the hope of finding a pass that would lead to the city. Half the men traveled by canoe, the rest on horseback. Once again disaster struck. All the canoes were lost in a flood and 30 Spaniards and all the expedition's porters died of disease. Berrío ordered all the horses to be killed (to discourage desertions) and the survivors continued in four improvised dugouts as far as the mouth of the Caroni River. There, like others before him, Berrío was assured by a local chief that El Dorado was only four days away. But he had had enough and abandoned the quest in favor of a return to safety.

Berrío's own exploring days were over. In 1593, however, he sent his lieutenant, Domingo de Vera, to the Orinoco once again. Vera returned after only four weeks with 17 sculptures of golden eagles and jackals. He told Berrío that he had found El Dorado, a cold, high city with temples full of gold in a new Inca Empire.

Some gullible people latched on to Vera's fanciful tale and embellished it. The number of sculptures trebled in some accounts. In others the "gilded man" himself was said to have sent tribute to Philip II. In reality, Vera had found nothing new, but had simply stolen the sculptures from Indian tribes. The evidence of his untruthfulness was that in 1596—this time with 500 men under his command—he made another foray into Guyana in search of the fabulous city. This time, no one survived.

By then the famous English soldier and explorer Sir Walter Raleigh (1552–1618) had got in on the act. In 1595, he sacked Trinidad and set off for Guyana, where he was welcomed as a liberator. He listened to the old stories about El Dorado, but was more interested in what he was told about a rich gold mine and what he was assured was a diamond-bearing mountain in the distance. Once again, the lure of treasure started to work its magic. Raleigh returned home to raise more men and make preparations for a second expedition—but now he was to fall a victim to royal power politics. After King James I succeeded Queen Elizabeth I on the English throne, James had Raleigh jailed in the Tower of London on suspicion of plotting treason. It was not until 1616 that the ageing explorer was released on parole to make one more expedition to Guyana. Too frail to venture up the Orinoco himself, he delegated command of the actual expedition to his son, Wat, and an adjutant called Laurence Keymis. They met the same fate as most of their predecessors. Wat was killed in a skirmish with the Spanish, while Keymis, after capturing a Spanish town, returned without having found a trace of any mine or diamond mountain. The vengeful James, faced with Spanish demands for reparations, had Raleigh executed.

The lure of El Dorado continued to exercise its magic. Five shiploads of French buccaneers, for instance, searched in vain for it in 1684, while a little more than a century later, Alexander von Humboldt, the celebrated German naturalist and explorer, fell under its spell. Even today, the legend persists. In 2002, an international team

Below: Hernán Cortés (1485–1547) arrives in Mexico in 1519. Like all his fellow conquistadors, Cortés was driven by the lust for treasure. He explained his need to the Aztecs by saying that he and his men "suffered from a disease of the heart which could only be cured by gold."

"To travel hopefully is a better thing than to arrive."

ROBERT LOUIS STEVENSON
"EL DORADO," 1881

Vm Gualtherus Ralegh, nauibus suis ad Insulam TRINI-
DAD appulisset, Hispanos in PVERTO DE LOS ESPAN-
NOLES, blandis verbis gestibusq, ad se inuitauit, & nō tan-
tum Insularum statum, sed & Hispanorum vires atque po-
tentiam ab eis explorauit, postea vero cognitis rebus omni-
bus, Capitaneum CALFIELD cum 100 armatis sibi adiunxit, & circa ve-
speram ciuitatem S. JOSEPHI, in qua regius Gubernator DON ANTHO-
NIO de BERREO erat, oppugnatam facilé superauit. Quo facto, dimisit o-
mnes qui in ciuitate erant, excepto solo BERREO quem cum socus captiuum
abduxit.   d 2

Above: A page from
Sir Walter Raleigh's
Discoverie of
Guiana shows the
explorer and his men
preparing to set off in
search of El Dorado
in 1595. Among the
marvels Raleigh
described was a tribe
of people "whose
heades appeare not
above their shoulders."

of explorers set off in search of the remains of the legendary city of gold deep in the heart of the Peruvian Amazon region in the unexplored jungle area along the basin of the Madre de Dios River. Their argument was that this was where a large body of Incas took refuge when they fled with their treasures ahead of the advancing Spanish conquerors back in 1532. They said that the sanctuary's existence had been confirmed by documents recently discovered in the archives of the Vatican in Rome. According to these, Jesuit missionaries found the city toward the end of the 16th century, but, with the agreement of the pope, decided to keep it secret for fear of encouraging a gold rush.

Elsewhere, on the banks of the Negro River in the central Amazon, archaeologists are retracing the route taken by Francisco de Orellana and his fellow conquistadors, the first Europeans to penetrate to the heart of the Amazon basin. In 1542, Orellana led an expedition deep into the rainforest in search of El Dorado. On his final return to Spain, he brought with him spellbinding tales of the unknown civilization he claimed to have located. When the Spanish returned in search of the wonders Orellana had described, however, they found nothing but a few scattered Indian settlements. Ever since, Orellana has been dismissed as a liar and a cheat, but now, so American experts believe, it looks as though he might have been telling the truth after all. Patient scientific spadework in the region has revealed that, far from always having been the home of small bands of wandering jungle Indians, the Amazon basin was once inhabited by prosperous farmers settled in large chiefdoms. This was just what Orellana had described all those centuries ago.

The new findings created a sensation, since they contradicted the hitherto accepted belief that, as productive as the Amazon rainforest might appear, the soil it stands in is totally unsuited to large-scale farming. If the soil could not support crops sufficient to feed a large number of people, so the argument ran, that would serve to put a cap on the population

Below: A contemporary
Spanish map of South
America shows the
conquistadors'
progress into the
continent's interior,
and Magellan's sea
route around the tip
to the Pacific.

and so make the emergence of a settled society impossible. The question the investigators now had to answer was how these contradictory views could be reconciled. The answer, it seemed, lay in the nature of the soil.

What the experts discovered was that the earth where they believed these early peoples lived was much blacker than the rainforest soil nearby. Detailed analysis showed that, though the two soils were basically the same, the samples from the settled areas contained an extra secret ingredient—a highly fertile dark loam, which Brazilians today call "*terra preta*" (black earth). It seems as though the ancient Amazonians must have literally transformed the earth beneath their feet, having somehow discovered how to mix organic waste with the soil and nurture it toward lasting productivity. This made possible the growth of permanent, sustained agriculture, which, in turn, fostered the development of a settled society.

Here, again, Orellana's accounts helped to shed light on the mystery. He noticed that the peoples of the region used fire to clear their fields—and research by two German soil experts, Bruno Glaser and Christoph Steiner, shows that "*terra preta*" is rich in charcoal. Both men believe that the charcoal acts to keep nutrients in the soil and so sustains its amazing fertility year after year. Indeed, "*terra preta*" may possess an even stranger ability. Almost as though it is alive, it appears to reproduce, since, as long as it is left undisturbed, it regenerates itself. Scientists think this may be down to the work of a biological cocktail of bacteria and fungi.

If this civilization was as flourishing as Orellana described, what happened to it? Why did it vanish so quickly? Tragically, the Spanish may have been the ones to trigger its rapid and catastrophic decline, destroying in just a few decades what had taken centuries to evolve. The visitors brought with them the germs of foreign diseases, such as smallpox, measles, and influenza, to which the local peoples had absolutely no inbuilt resistance. They perished in droves.

There is one final twist to the story. In "*terra preta*," the Amazonians could have left humankind a legacy far more valuable than all the gold the conquistadors were vainly seeking. If its secrets can be unlocked, it could be used to boost food production throughout the developing world. It might be the real El Dorado of the future.

Above: Sir Walter Raleigh with his son, Wat, in 1590. Raleigh's last expedition in search of El Dorado, in 1616, was his undoing. Wat died in a clash with the Spanish, while, on Walter's return to England, the furious King James I, faced with Spanish demands for reparation, had him executed.

WHAT HAPPENED TO NORTH AMERICA'S "LOST COLONY?"

Sometime between 1587 and 1590, the first English colony in North America disappeared almost without a trace. More than 100 men, women, and children seemingly vanished into thin air. Did they perish from cold and starvation? Did hostile Native Americans kill them? Or were they assimilated into a local Native American community? To this day, no one is sure exactly what happened to these first colonists. It is the earliest and probably the most baffling mystery in American history.

Above: Elizabeth I, who became Queen in 1558, was intrigued by the possibilities of establishing English colonies in the New World, provided that they would eventually pay rich dividends to the Tudor crown.

In the early 1580s, a handful of English adventurers began taking a keen interest in the possibility of setting up lasting settlements in the New World. The driving force behind the enterprise was Sir Walter Raleigh, a celebrated soldier of the day. He was also an accomplished poet, a famous wit, and a great favorite of Queen Elizabeth I. In April 1584, Raleigh dispatched two ships under the command of explorers Philip Amadas and Arthur Barlowe to search for a suitable site for settlement. Landfall was made on July 13 on what is now the North Carolina coast, a few miles north of Roanoke Island. A few days later, the English party encountered some friendly Native Americans from the island. Barlowe, with a few companions, went with them to meet with Wingina, the chief of the local Roanoke tribe. He, too, was welcoming and his subjects "gentle, loving, and faithfull." As for Roanoke Island itself, it seemed "a most pleasant and fertile ground, replenished with goodly Cedars, and divers other sweete woods, full of Corrants [grapes], flaxe, and many other notable commodities."

Having accomplished their mission, Barlowe and Amadas set sail for England that August armed with glowing reports of all that they had seen. What was more, they brought two local tribesmen, Wanchese and Manteo, back with them. Both Raleigh and Elizabeth were delighted by the success of the expedition, and the queen graciously agreed to

Opposite: This map of Roanoke Island was produced in Frankfurt, Germany, in 1590 to illustrate a book of great voyages. It was based on sketches made during the 1585 expedition, which was the first attempt to found an English colony there.

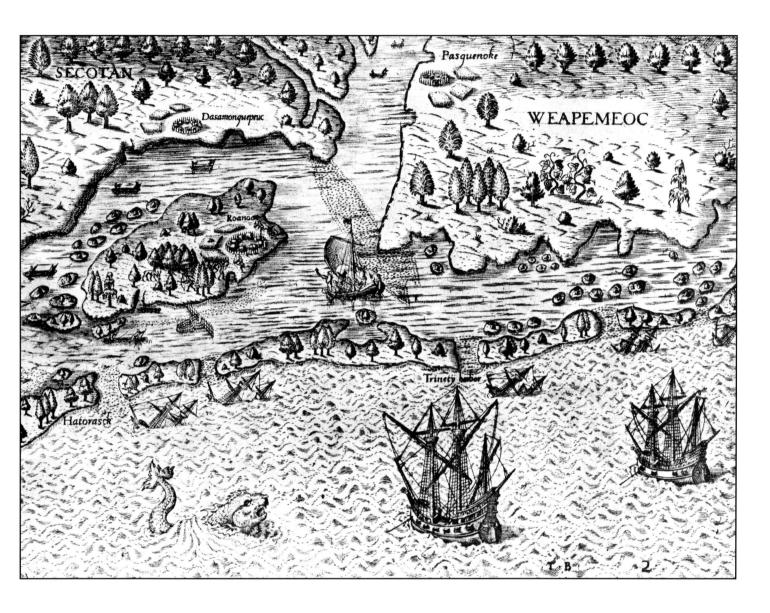

"It is the goodliest soil under the cope of Heaven; the most pleasing territory of the world; the continent is of a huge and unknown greatness, and very well peopled and towned, though Indianly."

GOVERNOR RALPH LANE IN A LETTER HOME TO SIR RICHARD GRENVILLE, 1585

THE LOST COLONY

naming the region Virginia in her honor—the unmarried Elizabeth was known as the "Virgin Queen." She granted Raleigh the right to all the territory he could occupy.

The next April, 1585, Sir Richard Grenville, Raleigh's cousin, led seven ships and 109 men across the Atlantic back to Roanoke. Wanchese and Manteo, both of whom by this time had learned to speak English, were on board. Local Native Americans received the arrivals hospitably and cooperated with them in the founding of their settlement. Ralph Lane, who was appointed governor of the fledgling colony by Grenville while he himself returned to England for more supplies, chose a spot at the northern end of the island to build a village, with a fort just to the east where there was a good anchorage. But, though the reports Grenville took back to England were optimistic, the settlement faced major problems that were to become apparent as winter drew on.

The settlers had arrived too late in the season for planting, so, when Grenville's return was delayed, they became dangerously dependent on maintaining good relations with the surrounding Native Americans. But the good relations turned to bad, with initial friction between the two turning into open warfare by the following spring. So, when Sir Francis Drake unexpectedly arrived at Roanoke on June 9, 1586, Lane and the settlers had their backs to the wall. Drake offered them a choice. He would leave behind him sufficient ships and supplies so that the settlers could stay at Roanoke for a further month and then, if they wished, sail for England, or he would take them all home with him immediately. After some indecision, Lane chose the latter and, on June 18, Drake sailed. Only days later, Grenville finally arrived to find the settlement abandoned. Unwilling to write off the venture completely, he left 15 men behind to hold the fort while he sailed home to get fresh instructions and reinforcements from Raleigh.

In May 1587 a fresh expedition left England. It was of a very different complexion to that of its predecessor, with married couples

Opposite (top): Elizabeth I, known affectionately as "Gloriana" and nicknamed the Virgin Queen, in all her court finery and splendor. She gave Sir Walter Raleigh, one of her favorite courtiers, permission to name Virginia after her. Opposite (bottom): Sir Francis Drake was another of Elizabeth's favorites. On his way back to England after circumnavigating the globe, he rescued the first Roanoke settlers in 1586 when their supply ships failed to arrive. Two years later, he played a major part in defending England against the might of the Spanish Armada.

English Colonies in America			The World
Amadas and Barlowe search for a suitable spot for the first English settlement in the New World, and decide on Roanoke Island, off the North Carolina coast. Virginia is claimed for England, and named in honour of Elizabeth I, the so-called Virgin Queen.	1584	1584	Elizabeth I takes an active role in helping the Protestant rebels of the Low Countries (modern-day Belgium and the Netherlands) against their king, Philip II of Spain.
Sir Richard Grenville leads an expedition of settlers to Roanoke Island. He leaves them there while he returns to England for supplies.	1585	1585	Spain founds the first permanent European settlement in the Philippines, at Cebu.
Sir Francis Drake arrives at Roanoke and evacuates the beleaguered community. Grenville returns, finds the settlement deserted, and leaves 15 men there to hold the fort.	1586	1586	The Moghal emperor of India, Akbar, conquers Kashmir. In Japan, the general Toyotomi Hideyoshi seizes power and sets out to unify the country.
John White arrives at Roanoke with 177 colonists. He finds the island deserted, save for the bones of one of the 15 men. The first English child born in the New World is called Virginia. Manteo is the first Native American to convert to Christianity. White sets sail for England for supplies.	1587	1587	Sir Francis Drake attacks the Spanish coast. Elizabeth I orders the execution of Mary, Queen of Scots, who, it is claimed, had plotted to assassinate her and support a Spanish invasion.
A Spanish scouting party puts in at Roanoke and finds it deserted.	1588	1588	Spain sends an invasion fleet against England, but the Armada is destroyed by the English and the weather.
John White finally returns to a deserted Roanoke.	1590		
		1591	Moroccan invaders destroy the Songhay Empire, taking its capital, Timbuktu.
Sir Francis Drake dies in the Caribbean.	1596		
		c.1600	Statue-building on Easter Island, in the Pacific, dies out, probably because of a dearth of natural resources.
The Virginia Company of London and Virginia Company of Plymouth are granted Royal Charters. The first Plymouth Company expedition is waylaid by the Spanish in the Caribbean.	1606	1606	The Portuguese "discover" the continent of Australia. The war between the great empires of the Habsburgs, rulers of the Holy Roman Empire, and the Ottomans comes to an end.
The first successful English colony is founded at Jamestown, Virginia, by John Smith of the London Company. His life is saved by the local chief's daughter, Pocahontas.	1607	1607	William Shakespeare finishes writing Antony and Cleopatra.

"If the English had tried to find a worse time to launch their settlements in the New World, they could not have done so."

DENNIS BLANTON, DIRECTOR OF THE WILLIAM AND MARY CENTER
FOR ARCHAEOLOGICAL RESEARCH, WRITING IN *W&M NEWS*, 1988

and children among its number. Raleigh appointed John White governor of the new "Cittie of Raleigh." Among the colonists were White's pregnant daughter Eleanor Dare, his son-in-law Annanias Dare, and the Native American tribesman Manteo. Where the earlier venture had been an attempt to secure an outpost and build the most basic infrastructure, this one carried the seeds of a real colony.

Opposite: The drawings inset on this early map of Virginia show Powhatan and Sasquesahanong "Indians." The Roanoke explorers had been welcomed by friendly Native Americans, but soon tensions started to develop between them and some of the local tribes. One of the clashes was sparked by the theft of a gold cup from the settlers.

Significantly, Raleigh decided to act on the information brought back to him by the Lane expedition that the Chesapeake Bay area on the mainland would be a more suitable site for a settlement, and told White to head for it. First, though, White put into Roanoke to pick up the 15 men Grenville had left behind him. Apart from the bones of one of them, clearly killed by the Native Americans, there was nothing to be found. Lane's fort had been razed to the ground, but the dwellings of the settlement, though abandoned, stood intact.

It was now late July, which is perhaps why White decided to stay put on Roanoke, rather than to push on to the mainland. Of course, the disappearance and presumed slaying of the 15 Englishmen was cause for concern. This was heightened when George Howe, one of the new arrivals, was found murdered. Manteo was on hand to explain that the Roanokes who had perpetrated the massacre and were responsible for Howe's death were living in the mainland village of Dasamonquepeuc. A punitive English raiding party promptly attacked the village. Only afterward did the English discover that the Roanokes had already fled the scene and that their victims were Croatoans, who were busy picking over the remains of the village. Manteo was apparently able to patch up relations, but it is possible that the incident caused lasting resentment.

A happier event occurred on August 18, when Eleanor Dare gave birth to a daughter. Named Virginia in honor of her birthplace, she was the first English child to be born in the New World. On August 27, Governor White set off on the long homeward voyage for supplies. Accounts differ as to the number of settlers he left behind, but there were at least 112 and maybe even a few more. Of these, 17 were women and 11 were children, including baby Virginia and another

Above: A Native American woman and child in the fields. The woman is carrying a water jug—probably to water newly planted seedlings—while the child is calling on the spirits for rain. The arrival of the main body of colonists coincided with three years of drought and consequent crop failure.

Above: This drawing of what the illustrator called a Native American "Festive Dance" was made in around 1590. The dance may have been celebrating the Green Corn or Harvest Festival.

infant born almost immediately after she was. White had taken every precaution he could to ensure the safety of all of them. A code had been devised for use if the settlers had to flee the island. They were to carve where they were going on a conspicuous tree. If such a move had to be made under duress, a distress signal in the form of a Maltese cross was to be carved over the name of the new location.

What White could not have anticipated, however, was open war with Spain, which delayed his return until 1590. He arrived at Roanoke on August 18, only to find that the houses had been torn down and the settlement surrounded "with a high pallisado of great trees... very fort-like." On one of the palisades, White found carved the word "CROATOAN," and the letters "CRO" on a nearby tree. There was no sign of a Maltese cross.

The inference White drew was that, for whatever reason, the settlers had relocated to the island home of Manteo's people to the south. The prevailing winds made it impossible for him to sail directly there, so the expedition first made for the West Indies for fresh supplies. There the ships were driven out into the Atlantic by a hurricane,

"If Virginia had but horses... and were inhabited by English, no realm in Christendom were comparable to it."

GOVERNOR RALPH LANE IN A LETTER HOME TO RICHARD GRENVILLE, 1585

leaving White no choice but to return to England. He was never able to raise the funds to make the trip to America again.

The first news of what might have happened at Roanoke did not come until after the setting-up of a new colony at Jamestown, Virginia, in 1607. The powerful Native American chieftain Powhatan apparently boasted of having slain a number of the Roanoke colonists, who had resettled with friendly tribes on the mainland along Chesapeake

Bay. Then, in 1709, the explorer John Lawson spent some time among the Hatteras people, descendants of the original Croatoan tribe. He wrote that "several of their ancestors were white people… the truth of which is confirmed by grey eyes being found… among these Indians and no others." In the 1880s, Hamilton MacMillan, who lived in southeastern North Carolina, claimed that the Pembroke Native Americans had fair eyes, light hair, and other characteristically European features.

Another theory was much more short-lived. In 1937, a mysterious stone was unearthed in a swamp some 60 miles (97km) west of Roanoke. Dubbed the Eleanor Dare Stone, it was covered with strange carvings that, when deciphered, seemed to be a message from Eleanor to her father, telling him that the settlers had fled the island after a Native American attack. Over the next three years, nearly 40 more stones were discovered. When pieced together they supposedly told the tale of the settlers' exploits up to Eleanor Dare's death in 1599. In 1940, though, a journalist exposed the whole thing as a hoax.

Recently, archaeological tree-ring analysis has suggested that climatic conditions may have at least contributed to whatever misfortune destroyed the colony. The analysis indicates that the whole area was hit by an exceptionally severe drought three years running from 1587. This would explain how food came to be in such desperately short supply. As for when the colony disappeared, Spanish records indicate that Roanoke was deserted when a scouting party put in there in the summer of 1588. The fact that the Spanish did not come across any physical remains makes it unlikely the settlers were attacked. What is more likely is that they turned to nearby Native Americans for help. Whatever might have befallen the men, it would have been usual for women and children simply to be assimilated into the tribe. But even today no one really knows what happened to the lost colonists of Roanoke Island. Probably no one ever will.

Right: What Thomas Hariot, a member of the 1585 expedition, called "Pomeiooc" was a Native American settlement enclosed by a palisade near the head of Middletown Creek. He described how the inhabitants "keepe their feasts and make good cheer together in the middle of the towne."

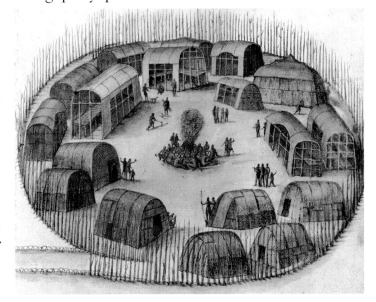

WHY DID JAPAN TURN ITS BACK ON THE WORLD?

In the early 17th century, all Christian missionaries and European traders were unceremoniously ejected from Japan by new, strong-arm rulers. At the same time, the Japanese themselves were prohibited from going abroad and Christian converts were massacred. Japan was to stay closed to the West for the next 200 years. What made Japan close itself off from the outside world?

In 1542 or 1543 a crew of Portuguese sailors taking a Chinese junk to Macao, on the estuary of the Canton River in China, were blown ashore by unfavorable winds on a Japanese island just off the port of Kyushu. They were the first Europeans to set foot in Japan, and brought with them the first muskets the Japanese had ever seen. They were followed in 1549 by a Portuguese vessel carrying three Jesuit missionaries, including the Spaniard Francis Xavier, and by another Portuguese sailing ship bound for the China coast that was wrecked on the shores of Kyushu. Thus, within a few short years, Christianity and guns arrived in Japan from the West.

By a happy coincidence, at least for the Portuguese, in 1549, the very same year, China banned all Japanese trading missions to its ports. The Portuguese were delighted to inherit the trade, bringing silks and medicines from Macao to Kyushu. The stage seemed set for the establishment of a fruitful relationship between Japan and Western Europe. The outcome, however, was not what might have been predicted. Just at the time that Renaissance Europe, emerging from the stagnation of the Middle Ages, discovered a new self-confidence and expressed it in looking outward, Japan was to turn inward and close itself off from the outside world.

Initially the Japanese people gave the Portuguese a warm welcome. Jesuit missions operated in Kyoto, Nagasaki, and other towns. Ladies of the imperial court at Kyoto helped to set a trend for conversion to Christianity, while the gilded youth of the capital took to wearing

Left: A scroll showing the leader Tokugawa Ieyasu, who believed Japanese Christians were plotting with foreigners to overthrow his government. He ordered the closure of all Christian churches as a reprisal. Opposite (top): A 1710 procession to Edo Castle, headquarters of the shogunate. By this time, Japanese isolation was complete. Opposite (bottom): A 1645 map shows how much the Japanese had learned from Jesuit missionaries about the world before isolation was imposed.

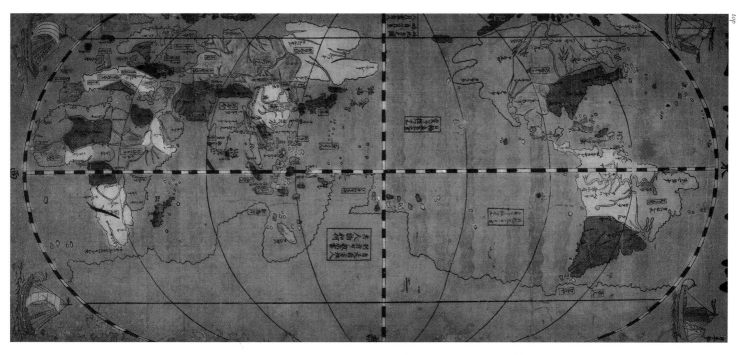

"In the rear of the soldiers, was a large number of the inhabitants… who gazed with intense curiosity, through the openings in the line of the military, upon the strange visitors from another hemisphere."

<small>COMMODORE PERRY'S JOURNAL ON HIS ARRIVAL IN JAPAN, 1854</small>

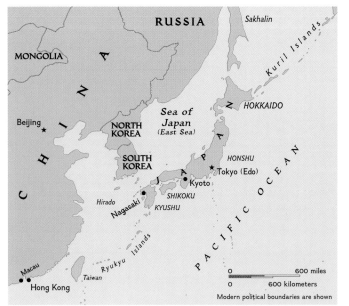

clothes in the Portuguese style and going around with rosaries and crucifixes. Several great feudal lords adopted the new religion and compelled the peasants on their lands to do likewise.

The reason for the conversions was not always simply religious. Impressed by the esteem in which Portuguese traders clearly held the missionaries, the Japanese concluded that the way to attract and conduct trade was through the Jesuits, who were quick to learn Japanese and were able to act as interpreters. The Jesuits were a new order, devoted to the expansion of the Catholic faith, and had been founded only a few decades earlier by a former Spanish soldier, Ignatius Loyola. They had a flexible, modern outlook and were open to scientific, medical, and technological knowledge. In 1580 they were put in charge of the administration of Nagasaki. Their efforts were supplemented by the arrival of missionaries of other orders from Spain. By 1600 there were about 300,000 Japanese Christians out of a total population of between 15 and 20 million.

Missionary work went hand in hand with Western commercial activity. Spanish traders, having gained control of Manila in the Philippines, arrived in Japan by the early 1600s, followed by the Dutch in 1609, and the English in 1613. None of the newcomers was able to gain a foothold on the Chinese coast. Instead they acted as intermediaries, bringing Chinese goods to Japan via Southeast Asia.

During the late 16th century, a bold and able military chief based in central Japan, Oda Nobunaga, acting in the name of the emperor (who had long been a symbolic, supposedly semi-divine, figurehead), had embarked upon a campaign to end nearly a century of civil war among contending feudal barons. After his murder in 1582, the campaign was continued by his most outstanding general, Toyotomi Hideyoshi, and after the latter's death in 1598, by Tokugawa Ieyasu, who had been the chief ally of both Nobunaga and Hideyoshi. Ieyasu's victory in the battle of Sekigahara in 1600 proved decisive, and his supremacy was confirmed by the emperor's bestowal on him of the title of shogun in

Opposite (top): Japanese geishas (courtesans) pictured in the mid-18th century. The highest-ranking ladies are pictured seated on the red carpet in the center. The ritualized geisha tradition was all part and parcel of the Japanese way of life that the country's rulers were determined to preserve. Opposite (bottom): National unity was not achieved quickly or easily. This scene from the Battle of Yashima shows what happened when central rule was weak and rival samurai clans fought bitterly for power.

Japan		The World	
The first Europeans set foot in Japan, soon followed by Jesuit missionaries.	1542/3	1542	*The Spaniard Juan Rodríguez Cabrillo is the first European in California.*
Portuguese ships start trading in Nagasaki, followed by other European traders.	1570	c.1575	*The Jesuits set up missions in southeastern and southwestern America.*
The leader Toyotomi Hideyoshi orders Christian priests to leave Japan.	1587	1588	*A Spanish invasion fleet, the Armada, is defeated by the British.*
Hideyoshi has succeeded in wiping out regional power bases and crystallizing the rigid class structure.	c.1590	c.1600	*The Maori in New Zealand enter their golden age.*
Hidetada takes power and begins wholesale persecution of Christians.	1616	1620	*The Pilgrim Fathers, English dissenters, arrive in America.*
Mass executions of Christians.	1622	1623	*Agents of the Dutch East India Company execute 10 English traders in Amboina, Southeast Asia.*
The Spanish are excluded from Japan.	1624		
A series of laws forbids the Japanese from going abroad.	1633–6		
All feudal lords are ordered to spend alternate years in the capital, Edo, to limit their independence.	1635	1635	*The French claim Guadeloupe in the Caribbean.*
The Portuguese are banned from Japan, now leaving only the Dutch.	1639	1637	*Tulip madness in the Netherlands causes an economic boom and bust.*
The Dutch are limited to the manmade isle of Deshima, off Nagasaki.	1641	1642	*The English Civil War between the Royalists and Parliamentarians, led by Cromwell, begins. Charles I is beheaded in 1649. The monarchy is re-established in 1660.*
Haiku poetry develops, and theater, painting, and fiction blossom.	c.1675		
The tight restriction on the import of books about the West is relaxed, leading to scientific advances.	1720	1721	*Walpole is Britain's first prime minister.*
A decade of crop failures causes an increase in peasant uprisings, and in the shogun's financial difficulties.	1830s	1783	*Britain acknowledges American independence.*
Commodore Matthew Perry arrives in Japan with a letter from the U.S. president asking for a commercial treaty. Treaties with Britain, Russia, and France follow.	1853	1842	*The British defeat China in the Opium War and gain Hong Kong as part of their settlement.*
		1859	*Charles Darwin publishes* On the Origin of Species.

1603. During this period of intensified civil war, the European musket proved an effective weapon, and the Christians were generally looked on with favor by Nobunaga, Hideyoshi, and Ieyasu.

By 1600, Japan had been transformed from a land divided by civil war and rebellion into a more or less unified state with a strong central government. But with increasing order also came a change of heart. In 1587, Toyotomi Hideyoshi had issued two decrees. The first ordered Christian priests to leave Japan, on the ground that they had stirred up the lower orders to attack Buddhist shrines and temples. The second prohibited feudal chiefs from encouraging mass conversions to Christianity.

Hideyoshi's abrupt about-face has never been adequately explained. It was rumored that he was disquieted by evidence that the Portuguese were selling young Japanese abroad as slaves. Another possible explanation is that Hideyoshi was concerned that Christianity would prove to be a source of national disunity on the eve of a projected Japanese invasion of Korea and China.

The new anti-Christian policy was not immediately enforced. Some Dominican and Franciscan friars preached openly (unlike the

Left: Dutch merchants taking their tribute to the shogun. This 18th-century print shows a procession taking place in around 1690, by which time the Dutch, ridiculed for their "barbarian" ways, were the only Europeans allowed a toe-hold in Japan. They were confined to a manmade island in Nagasaki harbor and allowed only two visiting ships every year.

Right: A hall in the
shogun's palace at
Edo (the former name
of Tokyo) as it was in
around 1690. By this
time, the Japanese
shoguns of the
Tokugawa family were
well established in
supreme power. They
had tamed the rival
samurai clans and
turned the emperor
into a puppet ruler
who had little if any
say in the way his
country was governed.

Jesuits) in defiance of Hideyoshi's decrees. But in 1597 the first executions were ordered by Hideyoshi. A total of 26 Christians—six Franciscans, three Jesuits, and the rest Japanese converts—were put to death at Nagasaki. In 1612 and then 1614, Hideyoshi's successor, Tokugawa Ieyasu, disturbed by rumors of a plot hatched by Japanese Christians to overthrow the government with the aid of foreign troops, issued two more edicts

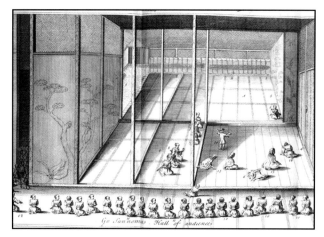

against Christianity. Later, Ieyasu ordered the demolition of Christian churches, and his successors required every Japanese person to register as a Buddhist.

Ieyasu died in 1616 and was succeeded by his son Hidetada, who immediately began a savage persecution of Christians. Special commissions hunted down thousands, who were subjected to brutal torture and execution, often by crucifixion. Mass executions in 1622–3 at Nagasaki, Miyako, and Edo became known as the Great Martyrdom. The English trader Richard Cocks was a disgusted witness of a public burning at the stake in 1623. He wrote later that he "saw fifty-five of them martyred at one time... Among them were little children of five or six years, burned alive in the arms of their mothers, who cried, 'Jesus, receive their souls.'"

The climax of the anti-Christian campaign occurred after a rebellion in late 1637 and early 1638 on the Shimabara peninsula, where the Christian peasantry took up arms against two oppressive feudal lords. After a heroic three-month defense, all 37,000 of the rebels were slaughtered. Their deaths marked the end of open Christian influence in Japan, although throughout the two subsequent centuries of Japanese isolation the Christian belief was kept alive by small bands of secret worshippers.

Long before the rebellion, the right of Westerners to trade with Japan had also been severely curtailed. In 1616 all trade at ports other than Nagasaki and Hirado was banned. Seven years later, a sorry record of commercial failure prompted the English to withdraw from their base at Hirado. The next year, after a dispute with the government, Spanish ships were excluded from Japanese waters. In 1639 the Portuguese were

"Unreasonable and wanton doctrines."

TOYOTOMI HIDEYOSHI ON CHRISTIANITY,
IN A LETTER TO THE PORTUGUESE VICEROY AT GOA, 1591

Above: A Japanese print showing the artist's impression of a Victorian English couple, dating from 1860, soon after the period of isolation came to a close.

accused, probably unjustly, of assisting the Shimabara rebels with guns.

Their punishment was swift. All Portuguese, missionaries and traders alike, were ordered to leave the country forthwith. They were warned that, if a Portuguese ship sailed into Japanese waters ever again, the crew would be executed and the cargo and ship burned. That was precisely what happened in 1640, when a ship arrived from Macao in the hope that the new shogun, Iemitsu, might have a change of heart. But the Portuguese were wrong, for Iemitsu showed little mercy. Only 13 crewmen were spared.

At the same time as the Portuguese were driven out, the Japanese themselves were forbidden to go abroad and were refused re-admission, or were executed, if they did. Japanese ships were restricted in size to fishing vessels and other small craft unsuitable for ocean voyages. By 1640 Japan had entered the era of *sakoku*, or "closed country." For the following two centuries its face was to stay turned away from the outside world.

Some historians disagree with the idea that Japan cut itself off from the world completely. For one thing, Japan maintained trading relations of a kind with its near neighbors, Korea and the Chinese dependency of the Ryukyu Islands. China itself lifted its 1549 ban on trade with Japan, and after 1600 Chinese ships were regular visitors to Nagasaki. It was the Europeans who were still being excluded, though, again, the ban was not total. The Dutch still had access to Japan—though they were confined to the manmade island of Deshima in Nagasaki harbor, where they were allowed to dock only two ships a year. There they remained for a further 200 years.

Though the Dutch influence over the Japanese was not great, their presence on Deshima did give rise to what became known as "Dutch studies." The import of

Below: American engineers demonstrate the marvels of steam to the Japanese in 1854. After the end of sakoku, Japan was quick to learn from other countries and embarked on a program of modernization.

Dutch books was permitted because, naturally enough, there was only a very small audience for publications in the Dutch language. Even so, Dutch-supplied books allowed a trickle of information from the West to get into Japan. As a result, there was a gradual growth of interest in Western scientific knowledge, especially anything that had to do with medicine. Japanese doctors in particular were ashamed to find their knowledge of anatomy proved wrong by Western books. Twelve schools of Western medicine were founded in Japan between 1786 and 1846 and, in the first three decades of the 19th century, books appeared on every branch of Western science, especially anatomy, map-making, and surveying. The first Dutch–Japanese dictionary was published in 1796.

Right: European toys on sale on a Japanese market stall around 1860. It was not long before Japan was copying many imported goods and selling them back to the West, undercutting their original manufacturers.

But an interest in Western things mostly came quite late in the era of *sakoku*, and it touched only the surface of Japanese society. Far more representative of Japanese opinion were the denouncers of "Dutch studies," who argued that "barbarian learning" would undermine Japanese civilization. The chief figure in the late 18th-century government, Matsudaira Sadanobu, collected Western books, but he wanted them kept away from the public, in whom they would encourage "idle curiosity" and "harmful ideas." One leading physician, while happy to gather knowledge from the Dutch, ridiculed them for urinating like dogs and wearing heels on their shoes because the backs of their feet did not reach the ground. Another scholar, Ohashi Totsuan, writing just before the end of *sakoku*, denounced Western learning for denying "the fundamentally hierarchical order of the universe and human society." In his opinion, it was no use saying that the idea was just to learn about technology from the West, because it was unsafe to drink from the side-streams of a river when the river itself was poisoned.

How is such deep-seated suspicion of and hostility to the West and Western ideas to be explained? China, which had introduced Buddhism

Above (top): A peaceful Japanese street scene at the start of the 19th century. Men carry baskets and buckets on yokes, while others transport passengers in sedan chairs.

Above (bottom): Opening up Japan to foreigners again did not go unopposed by traditionalists. Here a mob attacks the U.S. legation in 1861.

to Japan, was regarded as a superior society, worthy of emulation. Traditionally, China had been looked up to by the Japanese as "civilized" (*ka*), while other Asians, including themselves, were regarded as uncivilized. But as Japanese national pride grew in the 17th century, Japan came to think of itself as the equal of China in a world of "two heavens," in which the Europeans were the barbarians.

Some apparently minor factors may go some way to explain Japanese attitudes. Once Japanese craftsmen had learned the art of making muskets, the demand for European firearms fell away. And after the ban on overseas travel, the desire to learn Western methods of shipbuilding and navigation similarly diminished. But the real answer lay deeper, in the hold which Confucianism, an import from China, had gained over Japanese society.

Confucianism was a profoundly conservative ethical system, which taught people to be content with the station in life into which they were born, and established a fixed hierarchy of class divisions. At the top was the emperor, followed by his regent, the shogun, then the great landed feudal lords, then the military caste (samurai), then the peasants, then the urban artisans, and finally the merchants. Below them came the outcast class of cobblers and other leather workers, possibly the descendants of Korean prisoners. Farmers in Chinese and Japanese feudal society represented order and continuity; merchants constituted a threat to the system.

Western science in the age of the Scientific Revolution, with its emphasis on experimentation and observation of the natural world, expected to make discoveries that overthrew received notions. It thus presented a direct challenge to Confucianism. For the Japanese this meant continuing to keep European merchants well at bay, since, along with missionaries, they were the carriers of Western culture to Japan. Even before the persecutions of Christians began, Hideyoshi had explained to the Portuguese viceroy at Goa in a letter he wrote in 1591 that maintaining the new unity of Japan would require sticking firmly to traditional Japanese values and beliefs. Christian priests, he continued, expounded "unreasonable and wanton doctrines" that were likely "to bewitch our men and women." The same view was commonly held by Japanese Buddhists and scholars, one of whom wrote in 1620 that "Christianity elevated obedience to God above obedience to earthly rulers." This was completely contrary to the Confucian way of thinking.

There was also an understandable (and realistic) fear that Christian missions would prove to be the advance guard for Western empire-builders. Perhaps the most important reason for the continuance of *sakoku* was the growing Japanese awareness in the late 18th and early 19th centuries that Western power was increasingly extending into Asia, and that Japan was vulnerable to the more modern weapons that had now been developed by the West.

By the early 19th century, more and more Russian and British ships were to be seen in Japanese waters. Though trading rights continued to be withheld, the British defeat of China in the Opium War of 1839–42, and the leasing of Hong Kong to Britain, seemed to sound the death knell of Japanese isolation. It looked as if either Russia or Britain would be the first to breach Japan's walls. But when a Russian expedition reached Nagasaki in August, 1853, it found that it had been beaten to the prize by Commodore Matthew Perry's American squadron, called the "Black Ships" by the Japanese. A new power had announced its intentions in Asia and the walls of isolation were about to crumble.

In a sense, the reason why the Japanese withdrawal traditionally appears "mysterious" is that most Westerners failed to look at the Japanese experience as though they were looking through Japanese eyes. Japan progressed well enough on its own, isolated from the outside world. Towns increased in population and prosperity. Agricultural productivity improved and the nation remained self-sufficient in food. The development of silk manufacturing made the trade in Chinese silks carried via European ships less necessary. And the general standard of education was raised to a point that made the Japanese probably the best-read, most literate nation in the world.

Above all, the Japanese people lived in peace, except for local peasant uprisings, for two and a half centuries. Perhaps they missed out on the Scientific Revolution and the early Industrial Revolution. But when they needed to, the Japanese quickly caught up. Had the West not been rejected, Japan might have become just another European colony. Instead, it retained its national identity and integrity.

Below: A giant Buddha towers over a lake in Japan. Imported from China, Buddhism thrived in Japan. The strict rules Confucius laid down for ordering society, however, did not survive the re-establishment of contacts with the West.

WAS KING GEORGE III REALLY INSANE?

Ruler of Britain from 1760 to 1820, George III (1738–1820) has three claims to fame. First, though he was by no means solely to blame, he lost possession of America in 1783. Secondly, he tried, famously and unsuccessfully, to reassert royal power against that of parliament. But his third claim to fame is still the most controversial. Was he insane or not? The idea that George was mad—or at best suffered from protracted bouts of insanity—was accepted as the truth for 150 years. Then, modern medical research brought the whole notion into question.

For 150 years after George's death, historians were content to take the king's madness as read. The truth, though, was different. Doctors looking after the king at the time were far from sure that he was insane. Rather, most of them believed George was suffering from a physical, rather than a mental, disease, although, given the still primitive state of medical science, they had no idea what it could be. In fact, it seems as if not one of the bevy of doctors attending the king during his various bouts of mental derangement ever thought to examine him physically. Despite their belief that the illness was physical, it was George's mental symptoms that his doctors concentrated on at the expense of other possible causes: after all, it was the king's mental state that ultimately dictated whether or not he was fit to rule.

Some held that warning signs of temperamental instability were apparent early on in George's life. In a character sketch that he compiled in 1758, Lord Waldegrave wrote that the 20-year-old George had "a kind of unhappiness in his temper, which, if it be not conquered before it has taken too deep a root, will be a source of frequent anxiety." Later, it was supposed that a brief illness George had suffered from in 1765, aged only 26, was the first attack of "madness," even though no one supposed any such thing at the time.

Opposite: These portraits of George III and his wife, Queen Charlotte, date from 1773. The king is depicted as a Roman warrior, while the queen is set against a classical landscape. Both were great patrons of the arts. Left: Whether George III was mad or not is a question that still fascinates people. This is a scene from Alan Bennett's play The Madness of King George III. *George was treated just like this by his doctors.*

"I can never suppose this country so far lost to all ideas of self-importance as to be willing to grant America independence; if that could ever be adopted I shall despair of this country being ever preserved from a state of inferiority and consequently falling into a very low class among the European States."

GEORGE III IN A LETTER TO HIS PRIME MINISTER LORD NORTH, MARCH 7, 1780

Contemporaries instead concluded that George's symptoms—coughing with pain in the chest, some fever and fatigue—amounted to nothing more than a common cold. They were right.

Until relatively recently, though, historians and psychiatrists took the view that statements and incidents such as these supported the notion that George suffered from lifelong manic-depressive tendencies. These developed, under the stress of having to rule, into schizophrenia or a psychosis of some kind. But they would not have accepted the "madness" theory so easily, if at all, had they known the real facts. These were straightforward. George's first "loss of reason" occurred only in 1788, when he was 50, then, less seriously, in 1801 and 1804, and finally, as senility, in the last 10 years of his life.

The first illness started on October 17, 1788 at Windsor Castle, when George was struck by a "bilious attack," marked by fever, acute stomach pain, difficulty in breathing, aching joints, a body rash, and fever. Five days later delirium made its appearance in the form of incessant talkativeness and "an agitation and flurry of spirits, which hardly gives him any rest." Fanny Burney, a member of the royal court, confided to her diary that the king "spoke with a manner so uncommon, that a high fever alone could account for it; a rapidity, a hoarseness of voice, a volubility, an earnestness—a vehemence, rather—it startled me inexpressibly." The initial diagnosis was gout, but George knew that this was incorrect. He also knew that he was unable to control his speech and spoke of "a threat of the total breaking up of the constitution."

By November, as the delirium deepened, the doctors were talking of George's "alienation of mind." An equerry reported that the king talked of seeing Hanover, his ancestral home in Germany, "through Herschel's telescope" and that he "fancies London is drowned and orders his yacht to go there." As the Duke of Buckingham's brother reported, all the royal physicians agreed that the illness had been brought on by too much exercise outdoors in the cold. "The cause," he wrote, "…is the force of a humor which was beginning to show itself in the legs, when the king's imprudence drove it from thence into the bowels; and the medicines which they were obliged to use for the preservation of his life, have repelled it to the brain. The physicians are now endeavoring by warm baths, and by great warmth of covering, to bring it down again into the legs, which nature had originally pointed out as the best mode of discharge." Accordingly, medications to draw

Opposite: Novelist and diarist Fanny Burney served at the royal court as Second Keeper of the Robes for Queen Charlotte between 1786 and 1791. She was on the spot to record what happened when George III's illness first incapacitated him. She wrote how, on November 15, 1788, "the King, at dinner, had broken forth into positive delirium… and the Queen was so overpowered as to fall into violent hysteria."

*"The king...
kept talking
unceasingly,
his voice
was so lost in
hoarseness and
weakness, it was
tendered almost
inarticulate."*

DIARIST AND NOVELIST FANNY BURNEY,
NOVEMBER 5, 1788

George III		The World	
The future George III is born, son of Frederick, Prince of Wales and Augusta of Saxe-Coburg (grandson of George II).	1738		
		1739	The Persians under Nader Shah defeat the Moghal Emperor of India.
Frederick dies and George becomes heir to the throne.	1751	1751	Robert Clive captures the French colony of Arcot in India, tilting the balance of power in favor of British expansion.
George succeeds to the throne as George III on the death of George II.	1760		
		1763	The Treaties of Paris and Hubertusburg end the Seven Years' War, giving Britain large colonial gains.
He marries Charlotte of Mecklenburg-Strelitz; they later have 15 children.	1761		
		1769	Egypt breaks with the Ottoman Empire and claims independence.
George appoints Lord North as Prime Minister. He is a respected parliamentarian, regarded as a "safe pair of hands."	1770		
		1775	The American War of Independence begins.
Lord North's government falls, after disasters in North America.	1782		
George, disillusioned with North and his political ally Fox, appoints William Pitt the Younger as Prime Minister.	1783	1783	Britain recognizes the independence of the United States.
		1787	The first convicts are transported to Australia due to overcrowding in British prisons (prior to American independence, convicts had been transported there).
George suffers his first outbreak of "madness."	1788		
		1789	Revolution ends the monarchy in France.
		1791	Toussaint l'Ouverture leads a successful slave revolt in Haiti, in the Caribbean.
The king's prestige starts to benefit from the surge of national feeling that arises from resistance to the enemy in the wars with France.	c.1796		
		1799	The Rosetta stone is discovered in Egypt, making possible the translation of ancient Egyptian hieroglyphics.
George's second outbreak of illness occurs. A further outbreak follows three years later.	1801		
		1807	The Ottoman Turkish Sultan Selim III is deposed and replaced by Mustapha IV after a palace revolt by Janissary guards.
George's son is made regent, governing in his place due to the king's incapacity.	1811		
		1815	Britain and Prussia defeat the French under Napoleon at Waterloo.
George's wife Charlotte dies.	1818		
George III dies and the prince regent becomes king as George IV.	1820	1820	The Zulu nation achieves dominance in the Natal region of South Africa under their chief Shaka.

out the evil humors were prescribed: a "physic" of castor oil and senna; tartar emetic; blood-letting by cupping and leeches to the temples; and mustard plasters and other applications, called "blisters" because of the effect they had on the skin.

Though George improved physically, the delirium persisted and rumors of his insanity began to circulate. At the end of November, the king was moved against his will to the royal palace at Kew, just outside London. This was closer than Windsor for the concerned politicians at Westminster, and more convenient for the doctors. It was George's darkest hour. Kept apart from his wife for fear she would agitate him, and tied to his bed at night, his verbal ramblings—on one occasion he talked almost continuously for 19 hours—became indecent. The next month, Dr. Willis, the "keeper of a mad-house" in Lincolnshire, was called in. He brought a straitjacket and a number of "physical assistants" with him, because in his opinion the king needed "management." This

Left: William Pitt the Younger addresses the House of Commons. When George III appointed him Prime Minister in 1783 at the age of 24, Pitt became the youngest person ever to hold the post. He depended on royal favor to keep him in power, which was why George's 1788 illness was of great concern to him. At first, he did his best to cover up its seriousness, but was on the point of being forced to resign when the king made his dramatic recovery.

was shorthand for a regime that proved to be brutal in the extreme as far as the unfortunate king was concerned.

Meanwhile, at Westminster, with George showing no signs of recovery, a fierce political battle known as the Regency Crisis ensued. Night after night, parliament debated whether to pass a bill to authorize the Prince of Wales to preside over a council of regency and rule in his father's place. The Tory government under William Pitt the Younger was the king's creation. It was in their interest to argue that the king would recover, his illness being physical. The Whig opposition, pinning their hopes of office on the Prince of Wales, claimed that the insanity was permanent.

POLITICAL-CANDOUR, ie Coalition-Resolutions of June 14th 1805. Pro bono Publico.

The two chief physicians, Dr. Warren and Dr. Willis, also fell into dispute about the nature of the king's illness. Strangely, they adopted positions the exact opposite of what might have been expected. Dr. Warren, the physician, could find no physical cause and therefore leaned towards a diagnosis of "Original Madness" from which he could not predict recovery. He became the favorite doctor of the Whig opposition. Dr. Willis, who dealt in the "maniacal sciences," remained convinced that the cause was physical and predicted recovery. Pitt and the government championed him. Both doctors were accused of political bias, but the true reason that their opinions differed so markedly was mutual ignorance. As things turned out, Dr. Willis was unwittingly the wiser. By mid-February, the doctors united in the opinion that George had recovered sufficiently to be called convalescent. The medical bulletin for February 26 announced "an entire cessation of His Majesty's illness," and on March 10 the progress of the Regency Bill through parliament was halted. The political crisis and the king's illness were over.

All the same symptoms were present in the subsequent, much less virulent, attacks of 1801 and 1804: colic, constipation, hoarseness, muscular pain and weakness, sweating, sleeplessness, and delirium. On

A VOLUPTUARY under the horrors of Digestion.

each occasion the king's symptoms and his delirium grew stronger as his pulse-rate rose, sometimes to higher than 140 beats a minute. That was interpreted as a good sign, for although it put George's life in danger, it suggested that "fever" was the cause of the mental derangement. Each time, too, a period of convalescence was needed for the wasted and weakened George to recover full health—again, an argument against "insanity." Yet the belief persisted, eventually to be enshrined as historical fact.

Thanks, however, to Dr. Ida Macalpine and Dr. Richard Hunter, two British psychiatrists who started researching George III's "madness" in the 1960s, it is now generally accepted that the king's mental incapacity was almost certainly rooted in a recurrent and severe disorder of the nervous system. The culprit was porphyria, one of a group of diseases of the nervous system caused by an abnormal accumulation of toxic chemical substances in the body. The name comes from the Latin for "purple" and was given to the disease when it was identified in the 1930s because one of its characteristics is purple-colored urine and feces, caused by the overproduction of the purple-red pigments which give red blood its color. The result is literally the poisoning of the nervous system. George exhibited every one of the symptoms associated with the disease except hypertension (high blood pressure)—and that probably went undetected since doctors simply did not know how to measure blood pressure at the time. Though the color of the royal urine was noted by George's physicians, it suggested nothing to them.

Porphyria is an inherited condition. Sometimes it remains latent; when it is virulent it causes the severe illnesses suffered by George III. Nor was he history's sole royal victim. Mary, Queen of Scots, Queen Anne, Frederick the Great, and George IV, are now all believed to have suffered from the disease. The discovery has given a whole new twist to the phrase "born into the purple."

Opposite: George III in full military uniform. Though George's attempts to reassert royal power made him unpopular at the start of his reign, he became loved and admired by his people. When he died in 1820, long after being forced to allow his son to become Prince Regent by a recurrence of his illness, diarist Mrs Arbuthnot mourned that there had "sunk into a honored grave... the best king that ever adorned humanity." Left: A savage caricature of the plump Prince Regent when he was Prince of Wales. He was universally disliked.

"I do feel myself very ill, I am much weaker than I was, and I have prayed to God all night that I might die, or that He would save my reason."

GEORGE III, FEBRUARY 2, 1801

WAS NAPOLEON POISONED?

The bleak island of St. Helena in the south Atlantic was Napoleon's final place of exile. There, he was to die at the early age of 51, in May 1821. His death certificate said stomach cancer, but he had displayed none of the classic symptoms associated with the disease. Now, modern science suggests that it is highly likely that Napoleon was poisoned. But, if so, who was the poisoner, what was the poison, and how was it administered?

After his final defeat at the battle of Waterloo in June 1815, Napoleon Bonaparte found himself once more in exile on an island. Before Waterloo, the island of exile had been Elba, off the coast of Italy—but he had escaped. This time the island was remote St. Helena in the south Atlantic. Here, boredom was Napoleon's greatest enemy, for, though horseback rides helped to relieve the tedium, island life had little else to offer. Only one thing interested the former emperor, and that was himself. On the voyage out on a British frigate, he had contemplated suicide. To dissuade him, his close confidant, the Marquis de las Cases, remarked that reverses and endurance had their own "halo of glory." Things did not turn out that way.

Everywhere Napoleon looked, glimpses of British soldiers served to remind him of his fallen status, even though his jailers did their best to make his life comfortable. His residence at Longwood House, though no palace, provided him with splendid views of the sea and mountains. And for his comfort and pleasure, a bathroom, a room for books and maps, and a large drawing room had been added to it. He was allowed 20 servants to attend him. His cook prepared elaborate feats of patisserie—triumphal arches and amber palaces made of spun sugar. Meals were served on Sèvres porcelain and silver plate.

Napoleon continued to eat well until his last days. He died on May 5, 1821, at the age of 51. And he died fat. There was nothing extraordinary in that, except for the crucial fact that an autopsy found stomach cancer to have been the cause of death. Cancer, especially stomach cancer, is a

Left: A lonely Napoleon Bonaparte looks out over the Atlantic from the cliffs of St. Helena, his final place of exile. He had hoped to be allowed to settle in the United States, but his victorious enemies were determined to keep him under close guard so that he could never escape to threaten the peace again. Opposite: A Russian view of Napoleon's arrival on St. Helena. Though comfortable, the house that had been readied for him was by no means as grand as this print suggests. Nor was its architecture Russian.

"Shall I tell you the truth, Sir? Yes, Sir, shall I tell you the truth? I believe that you have received orders to kill me—yes, to kill me."

NAPOLEON TO THE BRITISH GOVERNOR OF ST. HELENA, SIR HUDSON LOWE, 1816

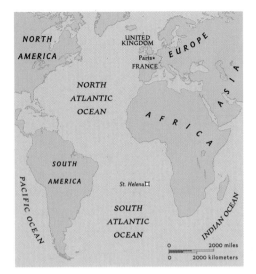

wasting disease. Ever since then, historians have been searching for some other explanation for his death. The true reason began to emerge only recently, when the Canadian Napoleonic scholar Ben Weider and Swedish toxicologist Sten Forshufvud organized the testing of five strands of Napoleon's hair. The strands had been taken from his head the day after he died and preserved ever since. Initial DNA testing proved that the hair definitely belonged to Napoleon. Then, through detailed scientific analysis, Weider and Forshufvud found what they believed to be the answer to the riddle of the emperor's death.

What was discovered in the hair was an abnormally high concentration of arsenic, five to 38 times normal amounts. Just as significant was the fluctuation in the amount of arsenic present in different portions of the hair, showing that the level of arsenic in Napoleon's system had varied considerably from day to day. On some days the level was close to the usual low level of 0.08 parts per million.

Opposite (top): The young Napoleon during his days as First Consul, the self-appointed leader of the French government. Opposite (bottom): A despondent Napoleon faces up to his first abdication in 1814. He escaped from his exile on Elba to regain power, but met his final defeat at the hands of the British and Prussians at Waterloo in 1815.

"Death is nothing, but to live defeated is to die every day."

NAPOLEON IN A LETTER TO GENERAL LAURISTON, 1804

But on others the reading soared—to as high as 51.2 and frequently over 20 parts per million.

The accuracy of the analysis was confirmed in 1995 by the poisons department of the Federal Bureau of Investigation in Washington. No expert has found other evidence to challenge the clear conclusion to which the figures point. Napoleon had been given dosages of arsenic of such high concentration and with such daily variation as to make it extremely unlikely that he was poisoned by his drinking water, his hair cream, or by emissions from the wallpaper in Longwood House—all previously favored theories. The poisoning must have been deliberate.

Convincing corroborative evidence came from a number of the emperor's companions on St. Helena, notably Louis Marchand,

Napoleon		France	
Napoleone Buonaparte (later Frenchified) is born in Ajaccio, Corsica. He attends military schools, then, aged 16, joins the army as a lieutenant.	1769		
		1789	The French Revolution begins as a mob storms the Bastille prison.
Now a captain, Napoleon wins a victory against the British at Toulon, and is rapidly promoted.	1793	1793	Louis XVI is guillotined, followed by all "enemies of the people." France declares war on Britain.
After putting down a Royalist uprising, Napoleon meets Josephine de Beauharnais, and is made commander-in-chief of the army.	1795	1795	A new constitution establishes the more moderate Directory in government.
Napoleon marries Josephine. He wins a string of victories over the Austrians.	1796	1796	France embarks on a period of European expansion.
Napoleon invades Egypt, but his supporting fleet is destroyed by Nelson. He flees, leaving his army behind.	1798	1798	France decides to attack Britain through her overseas territories, and heads for India by way of Egypt.
Napoleon overthrows the Directory and sets up a government called the Consulate, with himself as First Consul.	1799		
		1803	The French had bought Louisiana from Spain in 1800, hoping to build a French empire in the New World. But now France needs cash, and sells Louisiana to the U.S.A. After a brief, uneasy period of peace, Britain declares war on France again.
Napoleon proclaims himself emperor. The Code Napoléon he sets up remains the basis for many legal systems around the world.	1804		
Napoleon defeats Austria and Russia at Austerlitz.	1805		
		1808	After the French invasion of Spain, Britain sends troops and the Peninsular War begins. France now controls central Europe.
Now divorced, he marries Marie Louise, daughter of the Austrian emperor.	1810		
Napoleon makes a disastrous attempt at invading Russia.	1812		
Napoleon is defeated in the Battle of the Five Nations at Leipzig.	1813	1813	Britain, Prussia, Russia, Austria, and Sweden form a coalition against France.
Paris falls to the Allies, and Napoleon abdicates. He is sent into exile on Elba.	1814	1814	The Bourbon monarchy is restored.
He escapes from Elba and regains power. His defeat at Waterloo brings about his second abdication and exile.	1815	1815	The Congress of Vienna decides peace terms and draws up a new map of Europe.
Napoleon dies on St. Helena.	1821		

Napoleon's trusted servant and an intelligent and observant diarist. His journal's explosive significance did not become fully apparent until his notes and other records—which together record more than two dozen symptoms characteristic of arsenic poisoning—were put alongside the results of the hair analysis. What the comparison revealed was that the days on which Napoleon suffered from symptoms which now pointed to arsenic poisoning were precisely the days when the hair analysis showed that he had been given arsenic. The combined evidence led to one virtually sure conclusion. Napoleon had been murdered.

It was not arsenic alone, however, that killed the former emperor. He was murdered in two phases. Arsenic was first administered to him no later than June 1816 (one year after Waterloo), and the dosages continued down to his last days. The purpose behind this slow process was to make it appear that Napoleon had died of natural causes. The final phase did not start until the end of March 1821, when Dr. Antommarchi, the former emperor's personal physician, first tried to administer tartar emetic, a substance then used by doctors to force sick patients to vomit, to the reluctant Napoleon. Taken repeatedly over time, the emetic eats away at the stomach lining until the normal vomiting reflex is destroyed. Poison can then be administered without the stomach having the means to expel it. Napoleon was right to be cautious about taking it.

Finally, on March 22, 1821, Napoleon consented to taking the emetic when Antommarchi's urgings were fervently supported by one of Napoleon's own courtiers, the Comte de Montholon, who acted as his chamberlain. The emperor took two doses and Louis Marchand

Above: This watercolor of Longwood House, St. Helena, was painted by Louis Marchand, Napoleon's valet. Napoleon spent his days riding, walking in the grounds, gardening, and in dictating his memoirs to his companions. He hated the place. "I am in a tomb," he confided in despair to one of his followers in 1816. "I am only waiting for death to put an end to my torment."

> *"When I received the order to administer the calomel, I said that the Emperor had clearly told me he wanted no drink or potion that he had not approved."*
>
> NAPOLEON'S VALET LOUIS MARCHAND IN HIS JOURNAL, MAY 3, 1821

Above: Louis Marchand was a loyal, devoted valet, serving Napoleon like a son. Though his close contact with the emperor made him a natural suspect, historians agree that he had no motive to poison his master. Right: The Comte de Montholon had a Royalist background, no great liking for Napoleon, who had dismissed him from his diplomatic post, and was a beneficiary of Napoleon's will.

entered the results in his diary: "extremely violent" vomiting that brought up only a little mucus. Just over a month later, Napoleon was dosed with orgeat, a cooling mixture of orange flower water and bitter almonds (which contain prussic acid, the name given to the solution in water of hydrocyanic acid). Napoleon was told that he was being given it to help with his burning thirst—one of the characteristic symptoms of arsenic poisoning. The emperor's unquenchable thirst continued and he drank more and more of the orgeat. Dr. Antommarchi told him it was lemonade. "Lemonade!" Napoleon answered. "What a horrible preparation!"

Orgeat alone, though, was not the final agent of death. On May 3, Louis Marchand gave Napoleon some calomel dissolved in sweetened water. It was intended to relieve Napoleon of his constipation—another symptom of arsenic poisoning. The usual dosage was only one-quarter of a grain. Napoleon was given 10 grains. How could such a high dosage be explained?

That same afternoon, de Montholon had ordered Dr. Antommarchi to bring him a list of Napoleon's symptoms. Present at the discussions, also summoned by de Montholon, were Sir Hudson Lowe, the Governor of St. Helena, and two English doctors, Shortt and Mitchell. The English doctors prescribed 10 grains of calomel. Antommarchi protested that the emperor was too weak for such a dosage. De Montholon for some reason was allowed to act as arbiter, and he sided with the English. Louis Marchand takes up the story in his diary: "I finally agreed to mix the powder [calomel] with water and a little

"What a horrible preparation!"

NAPOLEON, ON BEING DOSED WITH ORGEAT, 1821

Left: Dr. Francesco Antommarchi, Napoleon's physician for the last 20 months of his life, catnaps while the dying ex-emperor lies unconscious. Count Bertrand, the court's Grand Marshal, recorded that Napoleon suffered "a total paralysis of the voluntary muscles. He could not even swallow." It took two days for him to finally die.

sugar... When the Emperor asked me for something to drink, I presented it to him as sweetened water. He opened his mouth, swallowed with difficulty, and even tried unsuccessfully to throw it up."

The two preparations of calomel and orgeat reacted together in Napoleon's stomach, turning into the lethal poison mercury cyanide. That evening, the crisis finally arrived. Napoleon's last hours were excruciatingly painful, though up until about three weeks before his death he had still been making jokes and singing popular Italian songs. Heavy sweats now meant a continual changing of the bedclothes. Then Napoleon fell into unconsciousness. He died just before 6 p.m. on the evening of May 5, 1821. Dr. Antommarchi performed the autopsy. He noticed the deep corrosion of the emperor's stomach lining and a growth at its base. His uncertain verdict was death from cancer. The doctor noticed something else that surprised him—Napoleon had almost no body hair. Antommarchi appears not to have known that loss of body hair is a typical symptom of arsenic poisoning.

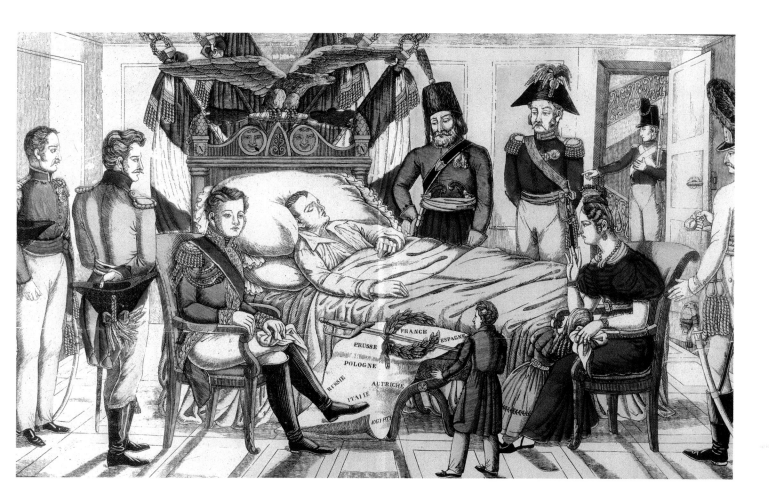

Above: The scene around Napoleon's deathbed. Among those standing is Sir Hudson Lowe (red uniform), the tough general the British had made governor of St. Helena. Whether Lowe was involved in any plot to kill the emperor is unproven, but Napoleon himself certainly believed that Lowe would welcome his death.

That Napoleon died an unnatural death is almost certain. But who murdered him? Whoever it was had to be on the island of St. Helena and close to Napoleon, probably actually living at Longwood House, not only during the emperor's last days, but also during the months and years preceding the murder. That narrows the list of suspects to just two: Louis Marchand and de Montholon. That so devoted a friend of Napoleon as Marchand should have betrayed him is highly unlikely. Montholon, on the other hand, may have harbored a grudge against his master. Five further items of evidence weigh heavily against him.

Though Napoleon ate the same food as everyone else at his table, he alone drank the Vin de Constance that was imported from South Africa especially for him. After February 1818, de Montholon was the emperor's wine steward. According to a member of Sir Hudson Lowe's staff, it was de Montholon who asked for the bitter almonds that were added to Napoleon's orgeat. In the quarrel between the doctors, two days before Napoleon's death, de Montholon sided with the English doctors,

who recommended treatment with 10 grains of calomel. De Montholon's 1848 memoirs are the only account to record that the emperor died emaciated. All the other journals and records say that he was fat. Did de Montholon lay a false trail in the hopes of lending credence to the story that Napoleon had died of cancer? And finally, by the terms of Napoleon's will, de Montholon received the largest share of his estate—what was for the times the vast sum of 2.2 million francs.

All of this evidence is, it must be stressed, circumstantial. There is no record of anyone's having witnessed the doctoring of Napoleon's wine. The case against de Montholon might leave a shadow of doubt in the minds of a jury in a court of law, but historians are bound by less exacting criteria. Somebody killed Napoleon and the most likely suspect is de Montholon. If de Montholon was, indeed, the guilty party, did he act on orders from a higher authority? Was he the agent of the British government and Louis XVIII of France? On one occasion Napoleon looked Sir Hudson Lowe in the eye and said, "Shall I tell you the truth, Sir? Yes, Sir, shall I tell you the truth? I believe that you have received orders to kill me—yes, to kill me."

It was, after all, Lowe who obtained the almonds for de Montholon. It was Lowe who, according to the diary of a Major Gorrequer, forced the doctors "to modify the conclusions of the autopsy report, because he did not want them to describe the changes they had noted in the liver." Lowe was not the kind of man to take such an important initiative independently: he must have been ordered to take these steps by his masters in the British government, probably with the connivance of the French king. The Bourbons and the English certainly had powerful reasons for wanting Napoleon to disappear from the scene. One thing is certain: this mystery will probably never be solved.

WHAT IS THE TRUTH BEHIND THE MYTH OF THE UNDERGROUND RAILROAD?

One of the most inspiring tales in U.S. history is the story of the Underground Railroad, which gave many slaves in the South the chance to find freedom. Historians now tell us that the Railroad was by no means as secret or as organized as the name suggests. There is also no evidence to support the existence of secret passageways or code words. In fact, the real stars of the story were the brave escaping slaves and the individuals who helped them.

Efforts to help escaping slaves seem to have begun toward the end of the 18th century. In 1786, no less a personage than George Washington was complaining about how one of his runaway slaves had been helped by a "society of Quakers, formed for such purposes." At this time, there were about 600,000 slaves in the United States; almost all of them were located in the Southern states. Though there were small slave populations in New York, New Jersey, and Pennsylvania, slavery never caught on in the North the way that it did farther south. Nearly all the Northern states had abolished slavery by 1804, and four years later the federal government outlawed the importing of slaves into the country. Nevertheless, the Southern enslaved African-American population continued to grow.

By 1860, some 4 million enslaved African Americans were living spread throughout the Southern states. Working mostly on large plantations, the majority of slaves were agricultural laborers, toiling literally from dawn to dusk in the fields. Many were involved in raising the cotton on which the economy of the South had increasingly come to depend.

Left: In this scene from Uncle Tom's Cabin *(1852), Harriet Beecher Stowe's anti-slavery novel, written in response to the 1850 Fugitive Slave Act, "Mas'r George" has come to give Tom a reading and writing lesson. In the South, teaching slaves to read was illegal. Opposite: Unloading a cargo of slaves fresh from their African homelands. Many did not survive the voyage across the Atlantic.*

"The public squares of half our great cities echo to the wail of families torn asunder at the auction-block."

ABOLITIONIST WENDELL PHILLIPS,
IN A SPEECH IN BOSTON, JANUARY 27, 1853

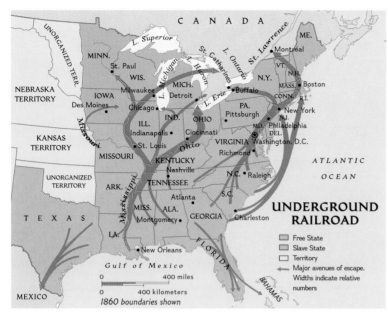

Slavery became a cherished, fervently defended Southern institution. As a result, tensions between free states and slave states grew and grew. The right to own slaves, the Southerners argued, was guaranteed in the United States Constitution and further strengthened when Congress passed the Fugitive Slave Act in 1793. This gave slave-owners the right to retrieve slave "property" from free states and territories. There was constant debate about whether or not to allow the extension of slavery into new states as they joined the Union. Many Northerners called for an end to slavery. It would take a civil war to settle the issue.

Opposite (top): In a poster illustrating a theatrical version of Uncle Tom's Cabin, *Eliza and her baby son escape the slave-hunters and cross the Ohio River to freedom. Opposite (below): The abolitionist John Brown, who was hanged in 1859 after an armed insurrection at Harpers Ferry in West Virginia.*

"Woman, did you raise your own children for the market? Did you raise them for the whipping post?"

ESCAPED SLAVE J. W. LOGUEN WRITING TO HIS FORMER OWNER, 1850

It was in this climate that what has become known as the Underground Railroad, a network of escape routes for fleeing slaves, was born. No one really knows for sure exactly how and when the term "Underground Railroad" originated. One commonly told story says that it was coined in the 1830s following a famous incident when a fugitive slave from Kentucky called Tice Davids was chased to the banks of the Ohio River by his irate owner. When Davids reached the far side of the river—and the free state of Ohio—he seemingly vanished before his owner's disbelieving eyes. The outraged owner explained on his return home empty-handed that it was as though Davids had "gone off on some underground road." What we do know is that the term first

The U.S.A.			The World
		1807	Britain makes the trade in slaves illegal, but the ownership of slaves continues.
Congress outlaws the importing of slaves.	1808		
Spain sells Florida to the U.S.A.	1819		
The Missouri Compromise sets limits on the spread of slavery into lands acquired in the Louisiana Purchase.	1820	1822	Freed slaves from the U.S. found the new state of Liberia on the west coast of Africa.
The Erie Canal is completed, connecting New York City and the Great Lakes.	1825	1833	Slavery is finally abolished in the British Empire.
Texas declares its independence from Mexico and becomes a republic.	1836	1840	Maori leaders in New Zealand sign the Treaty of Waitangi with the British government, giving the British sovereignty over the islands; but Maori resentment at the unfairness of the treaty soon leads to war.
Texas is admitted to the Union as the 28th state.	1845		
Mormons establish a religious colony in what is now Utah.	1847		
Thousands of prospectors start to arrive in California after gold is discovered.	1848	1848	Revolutions break out in France, Germany, Austria, and Hungary.
The second Fugitive Slave Act makes it illegal to help runaway slaves in the Northern states.	1850	1850	The 14-year Taiping rebellion erupts in China. Up to 50 million people die.
Kansas and Nebraska join the Union; the Kansas-Nebraska Act lets them choose whether or not to allow slavery.	1854	1857	Native Indian rulers and soldiers mutiny against British rule in India.
The famous abolitionist John Brown is executed in Virginia for trying to cause a slave rebellion.	1859	1861	20 million serfs (feudal slaves, bound to their master's land) are freed in Russia.
Confederate states secede from the Union after Abraham Lincoln's election, and the Civil War begins.	1861		
Lincoln issues the Emancipation Proclamation, which commits the federal government to freeing the slaves.	1863	1864	The practice of transporting British criminals to Australia is officially ended.
The Civil War ends with the surrender of the Confederates, and the 13th Amendment to the Constitution is ratified, abolishing slavery in the U.S. Lincoln is assassinated by an embittered pro-Southerner.	1865	1867	Karl Marx publishes **Das Kapital**, his classic analysis of the social and political effects of the capitalist system.

$150 REWARD

RANAWAY from the subscriber, on the night of the 2d instant, a negro man, who calls himself *Henry May*, about 22 years old, 5 feet 6 or 8 inches high, ordinary color, rather chunky built, bushy head, and has it divided mostly on one side, and keeps it very nicely combed; has been raised in the house, and is a first rate dining-room servant, and was in a tavern in Louisville for 18 months. I expect he is now in Louisville trying to make his escape to a free state, (in all probability to Cincinnati, Ohio.) Perhaps he may try to get employment on a steamboat. He is a good cook, and is handy in any capacity as a house servant. Had on when he left, a dark cassinett coatee, and dark striped cassinett pantaloons, new—he had other clothing. I will give $50 reward if taken in Louisvill; 100 dollars if taken one hundred miles from Louisville in this State, and 150 dollars if taken out of this State, and delivered to me, or secured in any jail so that I can get him again. WILLIAM BURKE.
Bardstown, Ky., September 3d, 1838.

Above: A poster offering a reward for the recapture of a runaway slave. Slave-owners frequently placed such advertisements in local newspapers. The rewards offered could run as high as $1,000, which was not that much to pay considering the amount of free labor a slave would be expected to provide over a lifetime.

appeared in print in the 1840s, and it was long after that—after the Civil War—that the railroad terminology started to be used. Escapees were called "passengers" or "parcels," the homes where they found shelter "stations" or "depots," and the people who helped them along the way "conductors." According to today's historians, it was from this language—and some colorful reminiscences written much later on in the 19th century—that the notion of a large, secret underground organization grew.

Far from being kept secret, however, details of escapes along the Underground Railroad were highly publicized in both North and South, though for different reasons. Northern abolitionists used the Underground Railroad to dramatize the evils of slavery. It naturally suited them to play up its size and effectiveness. Southern slave-owners publicized it to protest against Northerners ignoring the Fugitive Slave Acts, especially the one passed by Congress in 1850. This made it a federal crime to help slaves escape and required people to help the authorities catch and return slaves to their owners. From then on, individuals who harbored or fed escapees faced heavy fines and even imprisonment.

What today's historians also say is that African Americans were fleeing slavery in the South long before the Underground Railroad, in whatever form, came into existence. The difficulty in painting a truly accurate picture of the workings of the Railroad lies in separating fact from fiction, especially as what is known relies to a very large extent on oral histories passed through the generations.

What is certain is that brutal abuse and punishment plus endless hours of hard labor without any pay drove many slaves

Below: A slave auction room. To meet the growing demands of cotton and sugar growing, slave-owners in the South built up an active internal slave trade to shift surplus workers to where they were needed. New Orleans became the South's largest slave market, followed by Richmond, Natchez, and Charleston.

Right: A slave auction in progress. Slaves lived with the constant fear of being sold away from their families. This frequently happened after the death of a plantation owner, when the slaves could be sold off as part of the estate. Historians estimate that most slaves were sold at least once during their lifetime.

to risk their lives to escape. In 1844, runaway slave Henry Bibb wrote from safety in Canada to his former owner: "To be compelled to stand by and see you whip and slash my wife without mercy, when I could afford her no protection, not even by offering myself to suffer the lash in her place...This kind of treatment was what drove me from home and family, to seek a better home for them." The dream of personal freedom was also a powerful motivator. The orator and writer Frederick Douglass, the most prominent of all ex-slaves in the anti-slavery movement, wrote: "I hated slavery always, and my desire for freedom needed only a favorable breeze to fan it to a blaze at any moment."

In the past, historians of the Railroad may have concentrated on examining the complexities of the "secret" organization; but modern historians prefer to concentrate on the sheer individual courage it took to make a decision to escape. If a fleeing slave found help, this was usually only after the most dangerous part of the long journey in search of liberty had been completed. Most runaways, indeed, never made it to freedom. Many returned exhausted and hungry to their plantations

"What to the slave is your 4th of July? A day that reveals to him, more than all other days in the year, the gross injustice and cruelty to which he is the constant victim!"

FORMER SLAVE FREDERICK DOUGLASS, SPEECH IN ROCHESTER, NEW YORK, JULY 5, 1852

after a few days or weeks. Others were brought back in chains after their recapture by slave-catchers. The punishments such slaves faced on their return ranged from savage beatings to sale to another master and even death.

Strong, healthy young men were the most likely to strike out for freedom. Their escape routes naturally depended upon their starting point. Those in the Deep South might make for nearby Mexico, where slavery had been abolished in 1829, rather than undertake the long and dangerous journey north. Some runaways took refuge in cities such as Atlanta, Richmond, Baltimore, and New Orleans, where they could blend into the free black population. Not that free African Americans were always safe—sometimes slave-catchers captured them as well. But the majority of fugitives to reach the helping hands of the Underground Railroad came from Border States, such as Maryland, Delaware, and Missouri.

The first few miles of an escape were always the most hazardous. Slave-hunters using tracker dogs might be hard on the fugitives' heels as they fled north—avoiding roads and taking advantage of the natural protection offered by swamps, bayous, forests, and waterways. Most traveled on foot by night until they reached the loosely connected series of routes that stretched through the Border States. There are many theories connected with how the slaves, most of whom could not read—and so could not follow signposts—found their way along the routes and to the different safehouses. Some historians suggest that slaves knew through word of mouth that moss grows on the north side of trees, so they could have used that as a guide. A popular belief is that songs and spirituals such as "Follow the Drinking Gourd" carried vital information about finding freedom—it has been suggested that "drinking gourd" meant the Big Dipper constellation, of which the North Star is a part. Another belief is that safehouses were signaled by a quilt or lantern hanging outside a window, or by colored cloths being tied to a gatepost. There is no knowing if such stories are literally true. Historians need hard evidence, found in documents, before they will agree that something is fact. Legend—or folk "memory"—is not enough. Escapees' stories were not told or written down for publication until after the Civil War, when the runaways knew they were definitely free. Before that, they would not want to give away information that would lead to their capture or prevent the escape of others.

Opposite: Slaves on the move having been "sold South." Covering some 25 to 30 miles (40 to 48 kilometers) a day on foot, men, women, and even children marched in large groups known as "coffles."

Above: A woodcut taken from an 1833 book titled Scenes of American Wealth and Industry, *showing slaves working on a tobacco plantation. Tobacco was an important crop for the South, but it was cotton that became the economic king.*

What is likely is that some fugitives had prior knowledge, picked up on the slave grapevine, that could help to steer them into sympathetic hands. This is backed up by hard evidence. Quaker Levi Coffin, whose home in Newport, Indiana, became known as the "Grand Central Station" of the Underground Railroad, wrote in his 1876 reminiscences: "As it became more widely known on different routes that the slaves fleeing from bondage would find a welcome and shelter at our house and be forwarded safely on their journey, the number increased… I soon became extensively known to the friends of the slaves, at different points on the Ohio River, where fugitives generally crossed, to those northward of us on the various routes leading to Canada."

The bravery of individual "conductors" should not be overlooked. Some ventured into the South itself to rescue slaves. One such figure

"We have had two of the fugitive slaves who fled from bondage in a whaleboat… They have gone on to Canada, for they were afraid to remain anywhere within our glorious republic."

RACHEL GILPIN ROBINSON, WHOSE FAMILY RAN A SAFEHOUSE IN ROKEBY, VERMONT, 1844

was James Fairfield, who repeatedly posed as a slave trader, while in fact spiriting away slaves from under their owners' noses. John Parker of Ripley, Ohio, who was part black, crossed the Ohio River many times to guide fugitives out of Kentucky. Perhaps the most celebrated of all was the African American Harriet Ross Tubman, who in 1849 escaped from

"I never did more congenial, attractive, fascinating, and satisfactory work."

FREDERICK DOUGLASS, WRITING IN 1881 OF HIS DAYS WORKING ON THE UNDERGROUND RAILROAD

bondage in Maryland and then risked capture by making 19 secret journeys back to the South to lead as many as 300 captives to freedom. For her heroic efforts Tubman became known as the "Moses" who had led her people to the "Promised Land."

Some escapees showed equal personal resourcefulness, planning their flight using elaborate ruses and disguises. Women dressed as men and men as women. In 1848, Ellen Craft, a light-skinned slave, passed herself off as a white man and traveled by train and boat from Georgia to Philadelphia accompanied by her husband William, who posed as her servant. For his part, Frederick Douglass made his escape from Baltimore to New York by train disguised as a sailor and carrying forged papers provided by members of the Railroad.

In one of his autobiographies, Douglass admitted that, as a means of destroying slavery, the Underground Railroad "was like an attempt to bail out the ocean with a teaspoon." Of course, he was correct. The efforts of the Underground Railroad alone could never have brought slavery down, even though it is credited with helping thousands of slaves gain their freedom. But the Railroad's importance should never be underestimated. It is not about secret passageways or coded songs. It is about the coming together of like-minded people, regardless of color, to fight for basic human rights and liberties.

Above: Frederick Douglass, America's leading African-American abolitionist, escaped slavery after several failed attempts. Below left: Harriet Tubman, the Railroad's most celebrated "conductor," was born into slavery on a Maryland plantation. Despite the massive bounty on her head, she made 19 trips into the South to help others find freedom.

WHAT IS THE TRUTH BEHIND CUSTER'S "LAST STAND?"

The Battle of the Little Bighorn and Custer's "last stand" became part of the legend of the American West—a model of unselfish courage against overwhelming odds. But it seems from new research that Custer blundered into a massacre out of a reckless desire to keep the glory to himself, and that many of his men were gunned down by the superior marksmanship of the Native Americans while trying to run away. What is the real story behind the Battle of the Little Bighorn?

Above: A Native American painting shows Custer and Crazy Horse, the Sioux war chief at the Little Bighorn, engaging in single combat. But there is no evidence that the two ever fought like this. Opposite: From the start, Custer's Seventh Cavalry was thrown into confusion.

In a quiet river valley in southeastern Montana stands a battle monument to the soldiers who died in the most famous battle of the Indian Wars of the 19th century. The river is the Little Bighorn and the battle of 1876 to which it gave its name went down in history as the courageous "last stand" of Lieutenant-Colonel George Armstrong Custer and the regiment under his command, the Seventh Cavalry. For a century afterward, publishers and film producers told and retold the thrilling and tragic tale of this legendary hero of the American West, a do-or-die military commander whose reputation remained unsullied even in death.

But recent research has stripped the Battle of the Little Bighorn of its legendary status. No "last stand," it seems, ever took place. According to the research, "glory-hunter" Custer, impetuous as ever, lived up to his nickname. But on this occasion his dash for glory was a blunder. Custer's forces were routed in a flash, and over half the men of the Seventh Cavalry were sacrificed in a bungled attack that should never have been attempted. According to legend, Custer and his men, surrounded by Native Americans, formed a defensive circle and fought bravely, man to man, until the last soldier was killed. But oral evidence from the Native Americans themselves—long discounted—and recent archaeological discoveries on the battlefield, have led historians to revise the story.

"It was a terrible, terrible story, so different from the outcome we had hoped for."

LIEUTENANT JAMES BRADLEY, 1876

In the second half of the 19th century, the Native Americans of the Great Plains and the Rocky Mountain regions, who numbered about 250,000, presented an obstacle in the way of the ever-expanding white settlement of the West. Mounted on swift horses and well armed, the Native Americans were determined to defend their buffalo hunting grounds, which provided them with both food and clothing. In 1862 the Sioux went on the warpath, massacring and capturing men, women, and children. Native American warfare was more or less constant for the next quarter of a century.

The United States government entered into a treaty with the Native Americans of the Great Plains in 1868. The treaty guaranteed the part

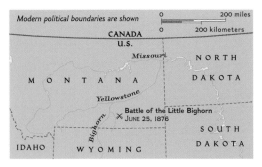

Modern political boundaries are shown

of South Dakota that lay to the west of the Missouri River as "Indian territory," reserved for their exclusive use for—in the words of the treaty—"as long as the grass shall grow." The wagon trail carrying white settlers through those lands was closed. But the treaty was honored for only six years, until it was undone by the discovery in 1874 of gold in the Black Hills. Within one year of the discovery, 11,000 prospectors had moved into the region; 25,000 more arrived the following year.

The Black Hills were inhabited by a number of Native American tribes, chiefly Sioux and Cheyenne, to whom they were sacred lands. To find new hunting grounds and escape from the invading white prospectors, a number of tribes moved to Montana. The government ordered them to return to their reservation. The Native Americans refused to leave. President Ulysses S. Grant offered to buy their land. That, too, they refused. They could not understand why, after centuries of roaming on the plains, they should be forced to live in one place all year round, to become farmers when they were hunters. Why should the earth, created for all men, be divided and allotted and sold for profit by the railroad companies who were pressing the American government to make war on them? Orders went out from the great Sioux chiefs, Crazy Horse and Sitting Bull, for all the lesser chiefs to gather their warriors together in the valley of the Little Bighorn.

With the situation in the Black Hills reaching crisis point, the stage was set for a showdown. Custer was sent to the Little Bighorn on a reconnaissance mission to scout for Native Americans. He wrote to his family: "I think the Seventh Cavalry may have its greatest campaign yet." Despite graduating bottom of his class from the West Point military academy, New York State, Custer had won golden opinions as the "Boy General" in the Union army during the Civil War, having been promoted to the temporary rank of major-general at an astonishingly young age. He was a swashbuckling commander who became famous for daredevil cavalry charges, personal courage, and tactical brilliance.

But he was also a controversial, wayward leader. Heavy casualties did not seem to bother him, and at times he seemed disdainful of army discipline. In October 1867 a court-martial stripped him of his command after convicting him of misusing army property and deserting

Right: A grieving officer mourns as the dead are gathered from the Little Bighorn battlefield to be buried where they fell. For some reason, though the Native Americans stripped and scalped the bodies of all the soldiers in uniform, Custer's corpse escaped the latter fate. Some historians think this was a mark of respect for his courage, while some say that, because his hair had been cut short for battle, he did not have enough hair to warrant scalping. Others believe that, since he had been wearing buckskins rather than regular military dress, the victorious tribesmen thought he was not a soldier.

"Hurrah, boys, we've got them."

CUSTER AT LITTLE BIGHORN, 1876

U.S.A.		The World
The Sioux tribe revolts in North Dakota and Minnesota.	1862 / 1862	The nationalist Giuseppe Garibaldi begins the process of Italian unification.
The U.S. army massacres 300 Cheyenne women and children at Sand Creek.	1864 / 1864	The U.S., British, French, and Dutch navies bombard the Japanese coast to force Japan to allow foreign trade.
The government signs a treaty with the Sioux and other Native Americans, establishing an "Indian territory" in South Dakota.	1868 / 1868	Russia begins its conquest of the independent Muslim states of Bokhara and Samarkand in Central Asia.
The wars between the Apache tribe and the U.S. army begin.	1871 / 1871	The German chancellor Bismarck achieves the unification of Germany.
War breaks out in California and Oregon with the Modoc tribe. When peace is made the following year, the Modocs are confined to a reservation.	1872 / 1872	Friedrich Nietzsche publishes his great work of philosophy, **The Birth of Tragedy**. It is the first element in his project of "re-evaluating all values."
The Comanche, Cheyenne, and Kiowa tribes in the southern plains fight white settlers in the Red River War.	1874 / 1874	Britain signs a peace treaty with the Ashanti king at the end of the Ashanti War on the Gold Coast of Africa.
Sioux, Cheyennes, and Araphoes unite to defend the Black Hills against white prospectors. The Battle of the Little Bighorn results.	1876 / 1876	The German Nikolaus Otto builds the first internal combustion engine, which will later be used to power cars, motorbikes and motorboats.
Chief Joseph leads the Nez Perces tribe in war against the U.S. army.	1877 / 1877	In Japan, the Satsuma rebellion breaks out against Western influence.
France presents the Statue of Liberty to the U.S.A.	1885 / 1885	The Land Act offers loans from the British government for Irish peasants to buy land from absentee landlords.
The U.S. army captures the Apache chief Geronimo in Mexico.	1886	
The government gives millions of acres of Native American land in Oklahoma to settlers.	1889 / 1889	Italy establishes her first colony, in Eritrea in east Africa.
The army massacres 350 Sioux at Wounded Knee.	1890 / 1890	Prospectors discover gold at Kalgoorlie in western Australia.
Ellis Island, New York City, opens as a transit center for huge numbers of immigrants arriving from Central and Eastern Europe.	1892	
	1893	Women are given the right to vote in New Zealand, the first country in the world to do so.

"Many, if not most, of our Indian Wars have had their origin in broken promises and acts of injustice."

his post without permission at Fort Wallace, in Kansas. Reinstated two months later, he led the Seventh Cavalry in the massacre of the Cheyenne at the Battle of the Washita, but was accused of abandoning a small detachment of his men, leaving them to be slaughtered. Among rank-and-file soldiers he was gaining a reputation for being mean and overbearing, with little regard for the welfare of his men. But to the general public, Custer's feats as an "Indian fighter" on the Great Plains, especially his victories over the Sioux, added luster to his Civil War reputation. By 1876, thanks to vast newspaper coverage of his various exploits and the timely publication of his autobiography, he was a romantic celebrity, revered and respected throughout the United States.

On May 17, 1876, the men of the Seventh Cavalry left Fort Abraham Lincoln and began their march to the Little Bighorn, 400 miles (650km) west. Custer was confident of victory. So was Sitting Bull, who in a prophetic vision had seen hundreds of U.S. soldiers falling head downward into his camp and being destroyed. On the sultry morning of Sunday, June 25, 1876, Custer looked down through borrowed field glasses on the valley where, from a high ridge, his scouts had pointed out to him a vast teepee encampment of thousands of Sioux and Cheyenne waiting to do battle.

Opposite: A Sioux war dance. Usually four days of such ceremonies were held before Native American tribesmen left their camps ready for battle. Right: Sitting Bull, head chief and holy man of the Sioux nation, united the Sioux, Cheyenne, and Arapho in defiance of U.S. government attempts to expel them from the sacred Black Hills and to move them forcibly from their ancestral homelands into reservations.

Their numbers, perhaps as many as 7,500, startled Custer. He had been given clear orders. He was to locate the encampment, report what he found to his superiors, and wait for reinforcements. But he disobeyed orders and prepared to attack. It was an astonishing decision, but also characteristic. He was known to his fellow officers as "lucky Custer," having escaped injury or death several times during the Civil War when horses were killed under him. The gods seemed to smile on him. Custer was bent on glory—the glory that would come to him if his regiment were to emerge victorious from the most daunting battle ever fought by U.S. soldiers against the Native Americans.

Custer divided the Seventh Cavalry into three groups. His own command, just 210 of them, were to attack the encampment from north of the Little Bighorn. The 174 soldiers under the command of Major Marcus Reno were to cross the river and attack from the south. Captain Frederick Benteen's detachment was positioned farther south to block any escape route for the Native Americans. Reno attacked first. It is at this point that legend and fact begin to diverge. According to the first movie made of the battle, called *Custer's Last Fight* (1912), Sitting Bull, the spiritual leader of his people and symbol of their resistance to the white man, fled in the face of Reno's assault. The movie told a story that white America believed—or wanted to believe. But evidence from the Native American side gave a different account. Sitting Bull remained to inspire his young braves. It was Reno who

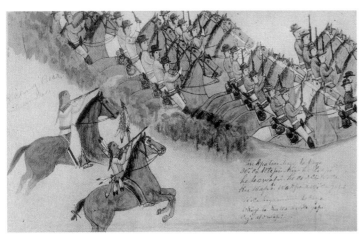

Above: On the verge of what he thought would be an easy victory, Custer ordered an immediate attack on the Sioux camp at the Little Bighorn. His rapid advance, against orders, put him far ahead of the other troops supposed to support him.

panicked and who led his men in a straggling retreat back across the Little Bighorn. A third of Reno's force was killed or wounded.

Unaware of the fate that had befallen Reno's force, Custer and his detachment proceeded along the northern ridge, discovering on the way that the encampment was even larger than he had imagined—three to four miles long (5–6.5km), much of it hidden by trees. Custer was still confident, but as the Native Americans donned battle dress and sang war songs, his scouts told him that all his men would die that day. Custer knew that he was facing the largest gathering of Native American warriors in North American history.

He dispatched a messenger to Benteen with a scrawled note asking him to send reinforcements. "Come on. Big village. Be quick. Bring [ammunition] packs." The messenger was the last man to leave Custer's presence, but he may not have been the last to see Custer alive. Private Peter Thompson described his last view of the dashing commander: "It being a very hot day," he wrote, "he was in his shirt sleeves; his buckskin pants tucked into his boots; his buckskin shirt fastened to the rear of his saddle; and a broad brimmed cream colored hat on his head, the brim of which was turned up on the right side and fastened by a small hook and eye to its crown. This gave him an opportunity to sight his rifle while riding." It is said, too, that Reno's men saw Custer wave his hat to them from his ridge before spurring his horse and riding out of sight. Maybe, maybe not: Reno's men were a long way off. But that last wave has endured in American memory as the symbolic snapshot of the Custer legend.

Reinforcements never came from Benteen, who chose instead to go to the aid of Reno's struggling troops. He has been criticized for negligence—as indeed Reno was at his later court-martials, the second of which ordered his dishonorable discharge from the army. But if Benteen had tried to carry out the order it is possible that his three companies would have been massacred on the way. Then Reno's weakened detachment would almost certainly have been completely

Above: Two Native American paintings show different stages of the rout of Major Marcus Reno and his troops. Contemptuous of Native American military prowess, Custer fatally divided his force into three before battle began.

overwhelmed, and when search parties arrived on the scene they would have found every single man of the Seventh Cavalry dead.

Benteen's own testimony to an 1879 Court of Inquiry into the battle was that, had he obeyed Custer's order, he would have been surrendering the lives of his men to the Sioux. "We were at their hearths and homes, their medicine was working well, and they were fighting for all the good God gives anyone to fight for," he said. If anyone was to blame for the disaster, Benteen believed it was Custer, the victim of his eagerness to win all the glory of victory for himself. Benteen wrote to his wife that Custer disobeyed the original order to make his reconnaissance and then wait for reinforcements "from the

"I think the Seventh Cavalry may have its greatest campaign yet."

LIEUTENANT-COLONEL GEORGE ARMSTRONG CUSTER, 1876

fact of not wanting any other command or body to have a finger in the pie—and thereby lost his life." President Grant concurred in that judgement. "I regard Custer's massacre as a sacrifice of troops," he told a reporter for the *New York Herald*, "brought on by Custer himself, that was wholly unnecessary, wholly unnecessary."

Neither Reno nor Benteen attempted to reach Custer with their men, and the legend has it that, left on his own, Custer charged. Yet

> ## *"We were at their hearths and homes, their medicine was working well, and they were fighting for all the good God gives anyone to fight for."*
>
> CAPTAIN BENTEEN'S TESTIMONY ABOUT THE NATIVE AMERICAN WARRIORS TO AN 1879 COURT OF INQUIRY

Above: A contemporary white American view of the "last stand." But the evidence suggests that no such heroic action took place.

according to the testimony of the Native Americans, he never attacked at all. And archaeological research has made discoveries that support their version of events. The litter of spent cartridge cases left on the battlefield indicates that Custer, for some inexplicable reason, possibly because he could not see precisely where the Native Americans were mustered in strength, further divided his small force into two sections, sending them in different directions. They never left the northern ridge overlooking the village. On the contrary, the Native Americans, abandoning their ponies, moved stealthily toward Custer under the cover of the woodland. When they fell upon him and his men, the Native Americans met with no coordinated defense. They surrounded Custer's troops in just a few minutes.

It is now that the "last stand" is supposed to have taken place. But there is no indication that a firm defensive position was ever held—indeed, the evidence suggests that a number of Custer's men, whose corpses were found hundreds of yards away from where the action had occurred, were in fact attempting to retreat or escape. None of them succeeded. The U.S. soldiers were outnumbered and outgunned by superior firepower—the Native Americans were armed with modern repeating rifles, whereas Custer's unfortunate troops were equipped only with single-shot Springfields.

The battle lasted for no more than a quarter of an hour. Native American and white testimony are in agreement that Custer's regiment—a ragbag of poor farmers and immigrants, badly trained, poor marksmen, some of them barely able to ride—simply fell apart. Two days after the rout, survivors from Reno's and Benteen's companies

Opposite: Within a year of the battle, the Sioux were defeated and broken. In 1877 Sitting Bull took refuge in Canada, where General Terry, in command of the Dakota territory, went to offer the chief a pardon in exchange for settling on a reservation. Though Sitting Bull angrily refused Terry's offer on this occasion, he was finally forced south to surrender in 1881.

made their way to the battlefield, where they saw strewn on the ground what one of the party called "the marble white bodies" of the dead. They buried the remains in shallow graves. With equal haste, the news reporters who had been nowhere near the battle began to manufacture the legend of the famous "last stand."

Custer's blunders had cost him his life, but now they gained him fame as a gallant victim of circumstance. Thousands saw the scene re-enacted in soldier-turned-actor "Buffalo" Bill's *Wild West Show*. Artists, novelists, and poets as eminent as Walt Whitman and Henry Wadsworth Longfellow got in on the act. In due course it was Hollywood—most memorably with Errol Flynn as a flamboyant Custer in *They Died With Their Boots On*—that kept the legend alive. There is little reason to believe that the revised historical record will succeed in killing it.

WHY DID THE
HINDENBURG EXPLODE?

*Above: Dr. Hugo
Eckener, chairman
of the Zeppelin
Company, and a
tourist postcard of the
Hindenburg cruising
serenely in flight.
Eckener had intended
to use nonflammable
helium in his new
dirigible. He was
forced to revert to
hydrogen when the
U.S.A., the sole source
of the gas, forbade
its sale to Nazi
Germany. Only U.S.
airships used helium
for lift.*

On the evening of May 6, 1937, the giant German airship *Hindenburg*, the luxury liner of the skies, was preparing to land on the last lap of its three-day transatlantic voyage from Frankfurt am Main, Germany, to Lakehurst, New Jersey. But what was just another routine flight became a catastrophe that would bring the age of airships to a tragic conclusion. In just 37 seconds, the mighty Zeppelin was consumed by a massive inferno that killed one-third of its passengers and crew. For many years, hydrogen, the highly flammable lighter-than-air gas that gave the *Hindenburg* the lift it needed to stay airborne, was held to blame. Today, however, new evidence is signalling a totally different conclusion.

Just three days earlier, the *Hindenburg* had slipped its moorings at Frankfurt am Main. There were 36 passengers and 61 crew on board. Passenger flights had begun the previous year, when the giant airship made a total of six round trips to Rio de Janeiro, Brazil, and ten to the U.S.A. This year, the *Hindenburg* made one further trip to Rio and back before setting off on its first North American crossing of the season. Luckily, the westbound passenger traffic was lighter than usual, although the return flight was fully booked. Up to this point, more than a thousand passengers had been carried across the Atlantic safely.

Flying the Atlantic by airship was expensive. The fare was $400 one way (roughly $5000 today) and $720 (roughly $9000) for a roundtrip ticket. For their money, though, the passengers enjoyed a level of luxury—in particular, space to move around in—that today's airline travelers can only dream of. The *Hindenburg* holds the record as the largest aircraft ever built. It was a staggering 804 feet (245 meters) long—more than three times the length of a modern Boeing 747. When fully loaded, it weighed 220 short tons (198 metric tons). The lifting power was provided by 7,062,100 million cubic feet (200,000 cubic meters) of hydrogen gas. The gas was housed in 16 cells contained

*Opposite: The mighty
Hindenburg was
consumed by a
gigantic ball of fire,
and—in less than
a minute—was
reduced to a heap of
smoldering wreckage.
Was the disaster the
result of hydrogen
being ignited by St.
Elmo's fire striking
the giant dirigible?
Or was it sabotage?
The mystery remained
unsolved until the
late 1990s, just over
50 years after the
fatal crash.*

"This is one of the worst catastrophes in the world! And it's a terrific crash, ladies and gentlemen. There's smoke and there's flames now, and the frame is crashing to the ground, not quite to the mooring mast."

EYEWITNESS REPORTER HERB MORRISON, MAY 6, 1937

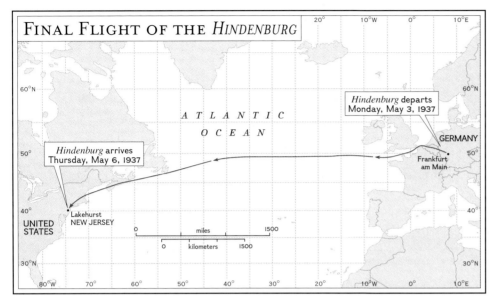

FINAL FLIGHT OF THE *HINDENBURG*

Hindenburg departs
Monday, May 3, 1937

GERMANY

Hindenburg arrives
Thursday, May 6, 1937

ATLANTIC
OCEAN

Frankfurt
am Main

Lakehurst
NEW JERSEY

UNITED
STATES

miles   1500

kilometers   1500

*Opposite (top): A
1936 propaganda
picture showing the
Hindenburg flying
over the Olympic
Stadium in Berlin.
The Nazis, who had
partly financed the
building of the giant
airship, were quick to
see how it could be
displayed as a prestige
symbol, though fear
of sabotage by the
regime's opponents at
home and abroad led
to security worries.
Opposite (below): A
1937 German air
mail poster showing
a sea plane and
a Zeppelin is
a celebration of
advances in aviation.*

within a structure of girders, which was covered by an outer envelope made of fabric. The dirigible was powered by four 1,100-horsepower diesel engines and had a top speed of 82 mph (132 km/h). Two large decks ran the width of the envelope. On the top deck, there was a lounge housing a baby grand piano made of lightweight aluminum; on the other side of that deck, there was a promenade with windows giving spectacular views.

The passenger cabins were located off a corridor running between the promenade and the lounge. Each cabin had a folding washbasin, while bathroom facilities and a shower were below on B deck, as were the kitchen and the crew's mess. B deck also had a smoking room. Considering the highly flammable nature of the hydrogen in the gas cells in the main part of the hull, this was startlingly risky. But the *Hindenburg's* designers had made sure there were strict safety precautions. Passengers wishing to smoke entered the smoking room through an airlock. The airlock was kept at a higher pressure than the air outside of it so that any escaping hydrogen could not leak into the cabin. The smoking room was equipped with just one electric cigar lighter, chained to the table. As a further precaution, all lighters and matches carried by passengers were impounded before every flight.

As with the *Hindenburg's* previous flights, the crossing went smoothly and safely, though strong headwinds slowed the giant airship down, delaying its arrival time at the Lakehurst Naval Air Station from 6 a.m. to 4 p.m. Gusting winds at Lakehurst then forced another three-hour delay, but, following a thunderstorm, they abated. Commander Charles Rosendahl, in charge of the Naval Air Station, radioed Max Pruss, the *Hindenburg's* captain: "Conditions definitely improved. Recommend earliest possible landing." Pruss stopped circling and started his approach to the Lakehurst field. As the *Hindenburg* maneuvered toward its mooring mast, he ordered the engines to be reversed to bring the ship to a stop. Then gas was vented off and water ballast dropped to

Manned Flight		The World	
Count Ferdinand von Zeppelin (1838–1917) tests his first airship.	1900		
		1901	The Commonwealth of Australia is created.
The Wright brothers make the world's first manned airplane flight.	1903		
		1905	Albert Einstein's Special Theory of Relativity is published.
Louis Blériot makes the first airplane flight across the English Channel.	1909		
Airplanes are first used militarily, in the Italian–Turkish War.	1911	1911	The Republic of China is declared by Sun Yat-sen's Revolutionary Alliance.
		1912	The Titanic sinks in the north Atlantic, killing 1,513.
The first scheduled passenger airplane service begins, in Florida.	1914	1914	The assassination of Archduke Franz Ferdinand in Sarajevo precipitates World War I, in which 9 million die.
Zeppelins launch the first ever bombing raids against an enemy capital, London.	1915	1917	The Russian Revolution overthrows the tsar. The U.S.A. enters World War I on the Allied side.
		1918	World War I ends with the surrender of Germany and its allies.
Britons Alcock and Brown make the first transatlantic airplane flight.	1919		
Britain's R38 airship crashes, killing 44.	1921	1921	The Irish Free State is created, after the country is divided in two.
The U.S.A.'s Shenandoah airship crashes, killing 14.	1925	1925	John Logie Baird transmits the first television picture in London.
American aviator Charles Lindbergh becomes the first man to fly an airplane solo across the Atlantic.	1927	1929	The Wall Street crash sparks off a global economic depression.
The U.S.A.'s Akron airship crashes.	1933	1933	Hitler becomes German chancellor.
The first air traffic control center opens in the U.S.A.	1935	1935	The anti-Jewish Nuremberg Laws are put into effect in Germany.
The Hindenburg begins the first scheduled passenger air service between Europe and the U.S.A.	1936	1936	Russian Communist leader Joseph Stalin launches show trials and mass purges in what was then the U.S.S.R.
The Hindenburg crashes, killing 36.	1937		
		1939	The German invasion of Poland signals the start of World War II.

bring the dirigible down to a height of 200 feet (60 meters). At this point, mooring lines were dropped to the ground crew in order for them to tow the airship into final position. The time was 7:25 p.m.

On the ground, eyewitness radio reporter Herb Morrison was making a recording of the landing for a future broadcast. As he was speaking, a few observers saw a small flame playing on the top of the airship's envelope near the tail fin. This, though, had scarcely a moment to register before all eyes were transfixed. The mighty *Hindenburg* was engulfed in a mass of flame and smoke that towered hundreds of feet into the skies. As the fire raced forward along the ship from the tail, the doomed airship sank tail first to the ground, its nose

"It's lightning! Jump!"

DIRECTOR OF FLIGHT OPERATIONS CAPTAIN ERNST LEHMANN, SECONDS INTO THE DISASTER

pointing briefly skyward before it, too, slumped to the earth. In just 37 seconds, the remains of the ship lay burning, the twisted skeleton of its framework the only thing visible through the inferno. The Lakehurst alarm siren sounded as passengers, aircrew, and ground crew jumped, stumbled, and ran for their lives. Of the 97 people on board, 62 of them, including Captain Pruss, managed to escape with their lives. Some jumped from the airship as it came crashing to the ground, hoping that the sandy field would cushion their fall. Others pushed through the tangle of blazing girders or forced their way through the fabric panels of the hull. One survivor slid down a white-hot wire in order to escape.

Even while the charred wreckage was still smoldering, postmortems into the cause of the disaster were starting. Pruss was convinced his dirigible had been sabotaged and that a passenger or disgruntled crewmember had planted a time bomb on board. As a potent symbol of Nazi propaganda, the *Hindenburg* could have been seen as a

prestigious target for someone who loathed Hitler's regime. But though the FBI investigated passengers, and threatening letters sent to Zeppelin officials, no confirming proof was found. Ultimately the official investigations into the disaster held by both the U.S. and German governments concluded that it was just a tragic accident. Somehow hydrogen had leaked from one of the gas cells toward the stern of the *Hindenburg* and then had been ignited by an electrical spark.

What caused the leak and the spark could not be proved. The favored theory was that a bracing wire might have snapped when the *Hindenburg* made its final turn toward its mooring mast and punctured a gas cell. Once the escaping hydrogen had mixed with the air, it would have needed only one spark to set it off, and that was probably provided by a rare natural phenomenon known as St. Elmo's fire. This is the name given to a static electrical discharge that is usually spotted around high objects, such as church steeples, during stormy weather.

Hydrogen, then, was held to blame. In the late 1990s, however, fresh research shed totally new light on the cause of the disaster, when Addison Bain, a retired NASA hydrogen specialist, and William D. Van Vorst, professor emeritus of chemical engineering at the University of California, published the results of their *Hindenburg* investigations. Working from newsreel evidence and eyewitness accounts, they showed

Above: As the massive Zeppelin burned, ground personnel raced to help the victims. In all, 36 people perished, plus two dogs. Among the fatalities was Captain Ernst Lehmann, director of flight operations for the Zeppelin Company.

that the way the fire on the *Hindenburg* behaved was completely uncharacteristic of the way hydrogen behaves when it is set on fire. Hydrogen flames rise upward, but in this instance the fire spread downward. Hydrogen burns without much of a visible flame, but eyewitnesses described the *Hindenburg* fire as being very colorful. Finally, the dirigible's gas cells were laced with garlic to permeate the hydrogen so the crew would be alerted to even the slightest gas leakage. No one on board had reported smelling even a whiff of garlic's strong odor during the flight.

If not hydrogen, what was to blame for the catastrophe? Having experimented with samples of the airship's outer covering, recovered after the accident, Bain argued that the solution used to waterproof the fabric was the real culprit. The chemical cocktail used consisted of iron oxide and cellulose acetate mixed with aluminum powder. This is very similar to a mixture used to power solid-fuel rockets. As Bain puts it, "the *Hindenburg* was literally painted with rocket fuel." He believes that an electrostatic discharge ignited the fabric near the tail fin, and all the fabric was quickly consumed by fire. The deaths were caused by jumping out of the airship, the crash itself, and burning diesel fuel.

A subsequent investigation into the Zeppelin archives in Germany revealed a report from Otto Beyersdorff, an electrical engineer hired as an investigator, which came to much the same conclusions. Though the Zeppelin Company never made the report public (it may well have

"Oh the humanity, and all the passengers screaming around here!" HERB MORRISON, MAY 6, 1937

been deliberately hushed up because its conclusions reflected poorly on German engineering skills), the chemical formula for the cover of the *Graf Zeppelin II*, under construction at the time, was hastily altered. It must have seemed better by far to blame hydrogen—or, as German air minister Hermann Goering put it, "It was decreed by an act of God."

> *"It burst into flames! It's fire and it's crashing! It's crashing terrible! Oh, my! Get out of the way, please! It's burning, bursting into flames and is falling on the mooring mast."*
>
> HERB MORRISON, MAY 6, 1937

Above: The disaster made headlines across the world. Strangely, one of the last in the German government to hear of the crash was the Nazi leader Adolf Hitler, who was asleep when the news reached Berlin— and his staff did not dare wake him.

Right: For the newsmen reporting the dirigible's arrival in the U.S.A., it was a routine job until the tragedy unfurled (top left to bottom right).

WAS THE ATTACK ON PEARL HARBOR REALLY A SURPRISE?

The Japanese attack on the U.S. Pacific Fleet at Pearl Harbor on December 7, 1941 fell like a bolt from the blue on the American people. Outraged and shocked, they rallied without hesitation to President Roosevelt's determined pledge to wreak revenge for this "day of infamy." But did Roosevelt and his closest advisors know about the impending attack and let it go ahead unhindered in order to pitchfork America into World War II?

Above: Admiral Kimmel, commander of the U.S. Pacific Fleet, was accused after Pearl Harbor of being unprepared for a Japanese attack. He always maintained that, had he been sent accurate information by Washington, he would not have been taken by surprise.

In the 1930s, relations between Japan and the United States steadily deteriorated. In 1931, Japan conquered Manchuria, until then a Chinese province, and in 1937 launched a full-scale invasion of the Chinese heartland itself. Evidence of Japanese atrocities in China caused revulsion in the U.S., to which was added growing apprehension when in 1940 Japan entered into a close military alliance with Hitler's Nazi Germany. By the fall of the following year, Hitler's seemingly unstoppable armed forces had overrun continental Europe and were smashing their way through the Soviet Union. Britain was undefeated, but had evacuated its troops from Greece and Crete, had suffered major defeats in North Africa, was facing a savage U-boat onslaught in the North Atlantic, and had been forced to deny the Far East promised reinforcements of warships, troops, and airplanes. Japan, meanwhile, had occupied French Indochina (later Vietnam) and was poised to plunder the riches of Southeast Asia.

The gravity of the world situation put intolerable strains on U.S. foreign policy. There was widespread aversion in the U.S. to getting involved in another European war, after the horrors of World War I. In fact, there was a strong belief in the virtues of isolationism, which was stridently proclaimed by the "America First" movement. President Roosevelt had acknowledged the strong antiwar sentiment by repeatedly pledging to keep his country out of war, but privately he was convinced that the survival of Britain and containment of Japan were vital to American interests.

Opposite: Struck by Japanese dive bombers, the destroyer U.S.S. Shaw burns after the explosion of her forward magazine, where her ammunition was kept. The attack came while the ship was moored in a floating dry dock at Pearl Harbor, and the blast, captured on film by a navy photographer, became one of the classic images of the Pacific war. Amazingly, the Shaw proved repairable. She was ready for action the following June.

"*Air raid on Pearl Harbor. This is not a drill.*"

EMERGENCY SIGNAL FROM ADMIRAL HUSBAND E. KIMMEL,
COMMANDER OF THE U.S. PACIFIC FLEET, DECEMBER 7, 1941

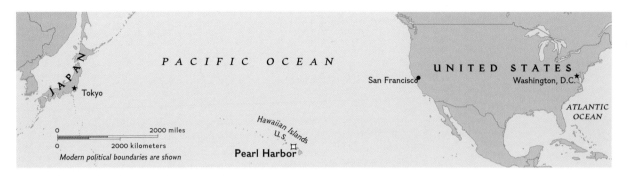

PACIFIC OCEAN

JAPAN

Tokyo

0   2000 miles

0   2000 kilometers

Modern political boundaries are shown

Hawaiian Islands
U.S.
Pearl Harbor

UNITED STATES

San Francisco

Washington, D.C.

ATLANTIC
OCEAN

*Right: In his planning of Pearl Harbor, Admiral Isoroku Yamamoto was inspired by a 1925 novel—*The Great Pacific War*—and the successful British air attack on the Italian fleet at Taranto the previous year. With the attack the Japanese scored a tremendous tactical success, but their decision not to launch a further strike to seek out and sink the absent U.S. aircraft carriers was to cost them dear.*

The alternative would be a nightmare future. Once it had crushed the Soviet Union, Germany would be able to concentrate all its military resources against Britain, which would either be forced to capitulate or be wiped out. This would make Hitler master of all Europe, with Africa, the Middle East, and Asia all the way to the borders of India at his feet. Meanwhile, a rampant Japan would sweep south to capture British, French, and Dutch possessions in Southeast Asia and on down to Australia and New Zealand, and west all the way to the great prize of British India. The entire Old World would be divided between Germany, Italy, and Japan, and the United States would be bottled up in the Americas.

To avoid this dire outcome, the Roosevelt administration had already risked conflict with Germany by providing Britain with "all aid short of war." This included the all-important Lend-Lease legislation, by which the U.S. continued to supply Britain with arms even though the British could no longer afford to pay their bills. As for Japan, the U.S. cut off shipments of oil and other raw materials vital for its economic survival. The decision put the two countries on a collision course. Last-minute diplomatic negotiations to stave off war appeared to be failing. On November 26, 1941, Secretary of State Cordell Hull warned the Japanese to get out of China and Indochina. Since there was no chance of Japan's complying, such a declaration made war inevitable. Indeed, the Japanese had already come to that conclusion.

There were two U.S. fleets in the Pacific theater—the Asiatic Fleet based on the Philippines, and the Pacific Fleet based on the Hawaiian island of Oahu, at Pearl Harbor. In October 1941 the Japanese general staff had given final approval to a plan devised by Admiral Isoroku Yamamoto, commander of the Japanese fleet, for a surprise attack on the U.S. Pacific Fleet at Pearl Harbor. The strategic thinking behind the

"Climb Mount Niitaka 1208."

ADMIRAL ISOROKU YAMAMOTO'S SIGNAL
TO HIS FLEET FOR THE ATTACK TO GO
AHEAD (12/08 WAS THE DATE IN JAPAN
WHEN IT WAS 12/07 IN HAWAII)

U.S.A.				The World
Gone with the Wind becomes the most successful film in U.S. box office history.	1939	1939		*Hitler invades Poland. Britain and France declare war on Germany.*
While still neutral, the U.S. helps Britain with armaments and vital supplies.	1940	1940		*Germany defeats France, but Britain's Royal Air Force beats the Germans in the Battle of Britain, securing Britain against invasion.*
The Japanese attack on Pearl Harbor brings the U.S. into the war.	Dec 1941	Jan 1942		*The Wannsee Conference in Berlin plans the Holocaust, in which 6 million Jews, Gypsies, and homosexuals will be killed.*
The Japanese invade the U.S.-occupied Philippines; U.S. General MacArthur vows to return.	May 1942	Apr 1942		*Allied shipping losses reach their peak in the war against the German U-boats in the Atlantic.*
In the turning-point of the Pacific war, the U.S. navy sinks four Japanese aircraft carriers in the Battle of Midway.	June 1942			
U.S. troops land in North Africa.	Nov 1942	Nov 1942		*The British defeat the Germans and Italians at El Alamein in North Africa.*
U.S. forces win control of Guadalcanal in the Solomon Islands, in the Pacific, after bitter fighting.	Feb 1943	Jan 1943		*German forces surrender at Stalingrad, Russia. This is the limit of the German advance in Russia and the turning-point of the war on the eastern front.*
U.S. troops invade Sicily and go on to land in Italy.	July 1943	Sept 1943		*Italy surrenders to the Allies; but the German armies and Italian fascists fight on in Italy, creating a virtual civil war as Italians fight on the Allied side, too.*
U.S. troops land in the Gilbert Islands, in the Pacific.	Nov 1943			
U.S. marines land on Guam in the Marianas Islands.	July 1944	June 1944		*D-Day: The Allied forces land in Normandy, starting the drive on Germany from the west.*
The Battle of the Bulge takes place: German forces counter-attack U.S. troops in the Ardennes, France.	Dec 1944	Jan 1945		*Auschwitz concentration camp is liberated by the advancing Russians.*
President Roosevelt dies and is replaced by Truman.	Apr 1945	Apr 1945		*The Russians reach Berlin, and Hitler commits suicide.*
The U.S. drops the first atom bombs on the Japanese cities of Hiroshima and Nagasaki, and Japan surrenders.	Aug 1945	May 1945		*Germany surrenders.*

"We have awakened a sleeping giant and have instilled in him a terrible resolve."

ADMIRAL YAMAMOTO AFTER THE ATTACK ON PEARL HARBOR

Right: U.S. Navy personnel, still in their Sunday dress uniforms, inspect the wreckage of a downed Japanese torpedo bomber in this imaginative reconstruction from the blockbusting movie Pearl Harbor. *The sinking battleship* Arizona *blazes in the background. The Japanese put 353 aircraft into the attack, manned by the finest pilots of their Imperial Navy.*

attack, which was to be supported by a simultaneous assault on the Philippines, was to deal with the only serious naval obstacle in the region to Japan's plans of conquest.

At the end of November, a huge Japanese taskforce, organized around 6 aircraft carriers with 24 supporting vessels and roving submarines, set out on this extraordinary mission. By dawn on December 7, the taskforce was about 200 miles (320km) north of Oahu. Just before 8 a.m. the Sunday quiet of Pearl Harbor was shattered by the first wave of 180 or more Japanese planes. While there were some 90 ships at anchor at Pearl Harbor, the main objective for the Japanese dive bombers and torpedo bombers were the eight American battleships, seven of them lined up together in the dock called Battleship Row—almost too good a target to miss. All were hit and three were sunk; the

U.S.S. *Arizona* alone went down with the loss of over 1,100 lives. A second wave of attacks followed half an hour later, and by 10 a.m. the Japanese planes were on their way back to their carriers, having given the Pacific Fleet a terrible mauling at very little cost to themselves. As well as sinking or severely damaging 21 warships, the Japanese invaders destroyed 188 American airplanes, most of them while they sat helplessly on the ground. It could have been much worse, however. The Japanese had expected also to have had three U.S. aircraft carriers in their sights, but two were at sea on an exercise and one was away for repairs.

Total U.S. casualties numbered 2,403 killed, with about half that number injured. Coordinated attacks on U.S. installations in the Philippines nearly wiped out the air force there, but it was the assault on Pearl Harbor that brought American minds into focus. President Roosevelt was immediately granted congressional approval for a declaration of war on Japan, and a few days later Germany honored its obligation to its ally by declaring war on the U.S. Four days after the attack on Pearl Harbor, the United States was fully committed to a world war on two fronts—against Germany and Italy in the European and North African theaters of war, and against Japan in the Pacific.

In retrospect, the attack on Pearl Harbor was a disastrous miscalculation by Japan, because it set its empire on the road to ruin. In its immediate aftermath, however, Japanese delight at having achieved such a stunning victory was mirrored by American despair at having suffered so calamitous a humiliation. Immediately, and on several more occasions during and shortly after the war, official investigations tried to unravel the mysteries surrounding the attack, and to apportion blame for what seemed an astonishing lack of foresight. Since everyone knew that war was likely to break out at any moment, how could Pearl Harbor not have been put on the highest defense alert?

The first investigation, completed just six weeks after the attack, pinned the blame on Rear Admiral Husband E. Kimmel and Lieutenant General Walter C. Short, the naval and army commanders in Hawaii, accusing them of "dereliction of duty." Kimmel and Short requested

Above: An Italian propaganda postcard celebrates the Japanese triumph at Pearl Harbor. Germany and Italy, Japan's Axis partners, fulfilled their treaty obligations by declaring war on the U.S.A. almost immediately after the attack.

Above: Lieutenant General Walter C. Short commanded the ground forces in Hawaii. Like Kimmel, he was forced to retire in disgrace. Both men claimed they had been kept in the dark.

court-martials so that they could defend themselves against the charge, but this was refused, and they were demoted and forced to retire. Subsequent investigations backtracked on making scapegoats of Kimmel and Short, as it became increasingly clear that they had been kept in the dark about much of the intelligence information that had been available in Washington. Their families' attempts to clear their names were successful in 2001, when a congressional commission posthumously restored their full military ranks.

There is no doubt whatever that, in the days leading up to December 7, a huge amount of intelligence information passed over Washington desks indicating that a Japanese attack was imminent, and that Pearl Harbor was its likely target. American and British code-breakers could easily read intercepted Japanese radio messages, and these messages made Japanese intentions clear. There are many examples, but the one most frequently quoted is a message of late November explaining that the signal to attack would be announced in a fake weather report from Tokyo, with "rain" meaning war and "east" meaning the U.S. On December 4, a U.S. intercept station picked up the weather report "East wind, rain." The fact that Kimmel and Short were not alerted to the danger can only be explained in one of two ways.

Different government and military departments received intelligence warnings, but inter-departmental communication in Washington was extremely poor. In particular, inter-service rivalry between the army and navy meant that neither would share its knowledge with the other. This version of events—that the U.S. got caught out by a combination of bureaucratic complacency and a failure to make proper use of intelligence information, remains broadly speaking the official position.

This version claims to account for even the most shocking examples of ineptitude that in fateful combination led to the disaster. For example, Short's aircraft were parked wingtip to wingtip in the middle of runways, making them sitting ducks for the Japanese. The reason for this was that Short thought that sabotage was the real threat he faced (Pearl Harbor was awash with Japanese spies), and that deploying his aircraft out in the open in a cluster made them a difficult target for would-be saboteurs.

Above: Attacking Pearl Harbor—a Japanese pilot's view. In response to a non-specific war alert warning, Short had ordered his aircraft out from cover into the open, where they could be guarded more easily against sabotage. The Army Air Corps lost 126 aircraft damaged and 77 destroyed, many on the ground.

Then there is all the confusion surrounding the last-minute intercept that revealed Japanese intentions. Late on December 6, American code-breakers intercepted a 14-part message to the Japanese Embassy in Washington, deciphered the first 13 parts, and passed them on to President Roosevelt and Secretary Hull. The message made clear that an attack was imminent, but not the target. The next morning at about 9 a.m. (4 a.m. in Hawaii) a transcription of the final part of the intercept reached the White House, containing an instruction to break off diplomatic relations with the U.S. Then an hour later another message was deciphered instructing the embassy to deliver the main message at 1 p.m. (8 a.m. in Hawaii).

The significance of this for Pearl Harbor was seized upon, since it seemed to imply an early-morning attack. The War Department attempted to alert Short, but because radio contact was temporarily broken it did so by commercial telegram. The telegram arrived about 20 minutes before the attack began, but it was seven hours before it was decoded and finally delivered. Another blunder was made on Oahu at 7:02 a.m., when two operators at the northern shore radar station picked up the first of the approaching Japanese planes and relayed their sightings to a junior officer. He disregarded the report because he thought the sightings were of a squadron of American B-17s expected to be flying in from the west coast of America. The long chain of misfortune and human error led remorselessly to disaster.

The official version of events is strongly challenged by an alternative explanation: namely that President Roosevelt and those around him were fully aware that the attack on Pearl Harbor was coming. According to this reading of events, there is abundant evidence that

Left: Battling with the fires at Pearl Harbor after the Japanese air strikes had been completed. Both Kimmel and Short had repeatedly complained that they lacked modern equipment to defend the base. That June, Kimmel had told President Roosevelt himself that "because of the deficiencies of Pearl Harbor as a fleet base… the only answer was to have the fleet at sea if the Japs ever attacked."

Above: President Roosevelt delivers his "day of infamy" address to Congress. When reading a decoded Japanese signal the night before the attack, he reportedly exclaimed, "This means war!"

Roosevelt wanted to bring the U.S. into the war against Nazi Germany at the earliest possible moment. But he knew he could not do so unless the American people were united in believing that there was no alternative to war. And the only thing that could unite the people would be a serious act of aggression against the United States.

Roosevelt's attempts to provoke Hitler into declaring war by blatantly siding with Britain had failed, so he laid a trap for Hitler's Japanese allies. First he goaded them into attacking (the Hull message was intended to be the final, unacceptable insult to Japanese honor), and then he made sure that the attack succeeded by keeping Kimmel and Short in the dark. The reason he wanted the attack to succeed was that only if Hitler thought the U.S. had been seriously weakened would he honor his agreement with Japan to declare war. In other words, Roosevelt conspired with his closest advisors—who must have known what was afoot—to sacrifice lives at Pearl Harbor (not to mention the reputations of Kimmel and Short) in a Machiavellian scheme to embroil the nation in war with Germany.

Opposite: Looking toward Pearl Harbor on Oahu. It was near this spot that the Americans sited their primitive radar station to warn them of any likely air attack. Unfortunately, the station was manned only part-time, and the report it sent in about the approaching unidentified aircraft was disregarded, since the Japanese air strike almost exactly coincided with the expected arrival of U.S. B-17 bomber reinforcements from the mainland.

"A Japanese attack upon the United States was a vast simplification of [America's] problems and their duty."

SIR WINSTON CHURCHILL, *THE GRAND ALLIANCE*, 1950

As to why Roosevelt would do such a thing, the conspiracy argument diverges on this. Most argue that Roosevelt was so aghast at the prospect of a world dominated by Germany and Japan that he was prepared to do absolutely anything to enlist the might of America in the struggle to prevent it from happening. If the only way of achieving his aim was to sacrifice Pearl Harbor, then Pearl Harbor had to be sacrificed. There are some, however, who are convinced that Roosevelt

was secretly a Communist and wanted to drag the U.S. into a war with Germany in order to save the Soviet Union from defeat. This accusation sometimes gets tangled up with the even weirder charge that the American president was spearheading a plot by Freemasons to establish a sinister world government.

Leaving aside such wild charges against President Roosevelt, the question of what he did or did not know on the eve of the attack on Pearl Harbor must remain an open question. What is not in doubt is that, for whatever reason, the Americans were not on the alert for a Japanese attack. Perhaps they should have recalled that Japan had begun its war against Russia in 1904 with just such an attack—the devastating surprise strike against the key Russian base of Port Arthur. The consequences of Pearl Harbor, though, were clear-cut. The entry of the U.S. into World War II made the defeat of the Axis powers inevitable.

DID LEE HARVEY OSWALD SHOOT PRESIDENT KENNEDY?

It seemed like an open-and-shut case. The Dallas police had got their man and the evidence against him appeared overwhelming. The doubts started when Lee Harvey Oswald was gunned down while in police custody before he actually could be interrogated fully, let alone tried. As more and more contradictions came to light, disbelief in the official version of events grew. Forty years later, new conspiracy theories are still appearing.

The assassination of President John F. Kennedy in Dealey Plaza, Dallas, on November 22, 1963, is one of modern history's most enduring mysteries. Although Lee Harvey Oswald, the alleged assassin, was arrested within 90 minutes of the killing, the slaying has often been described as the greatest unsolved crime in American history.

Initially, the facts seemed clear enough. In the late morning of that sunny November day, President Kennedy's open-topped presidential limousine was leading a motorcade through Dealey Plaza on its way to the Dallas Trade Mart, where the President was due to lunch with a group of prominent local supporters. It was traveling almost at walking pace, so that the President, the First Lady, and fellow passengers John F. Connally, Governor of Texas, and his wife, could be seen clearly by the welcoming crowds. Nellie Connally commented to the President on the warmth of the reception: "Mr. President, you can't say Dallas doesn't love you!"

Then, as the limousine turned onto Houston Street and neared the building housing the Texas School Book Depository, shots rang out. The President grabbed at his throat and slumped left toward his wife. Governor Connally, who had also been hit, collapsed. As a Secret Service agent jumped on board to shield the President and the First Lady with his body, the limousine sped off toward the emergency room

Left: A reconstruction of what President Kennedy's assassin might have seen through his telescopic sight. Opposite: The President's state funeral. After the assassination, Jackie Kennedy blamed "some dirty little Communist" for her husband's death.

"I myself believe that some individuals in scattered parts of the federal government either contributed to the conspiracy, or at a minimum were knowledgeable of it and contributed wittingly to a cover-up of the crime."

PETER DALE SCOTT, *DEEP POLITICS AND THE DEATH OF JFK*, 1993

Above: The Kennedy family in 1938. John F. Kennedy is standing in the center back, next to his mother. His father, Joe, is seated in the center. Opposite (top): John and Jackie Kennedy, with their two children, pose after Easter Sunday service. Opposite (below): John F. Kennedy, at 43 the U.S.'s youngest ever elected president.

of the Parkland Memorial Hospital. There, half an hour later, the President was pronounced dead.

Meanwhile, Dallas police officers had started questioning eyewitnesses and then as a result stormed into the Book Depository building. There, on the sixth floor, they found evidence of a sniper's perch. By a window that overlooked the plaza, they discovered three spent rifle cartridges and a bag. Then the officers spotted a 6.5mm Mannlicher-Carcano rifle that had been concealed hastily behind some book boxes near the staircase. Forensic testing was to detect some finger- and palmprints on it. Later, these were to be proved to match those of Lee Harvey Oswald, a low-level clerk in the Depository.

A bare half-hour after the search, Lee Harvey Oswald had been arrested. Initially, he was held in connection with the slaying of police officer J.D. Tippitt, who had randomly stopped Oswald for questioning as he had been walking down a nearby street shortly after the assassination. But, immediately, his interrogators shifted to the killing of the President. By 2:30 that afternoon, J. Edgar Hoover, Director General of the F.B.I., was confident enough to telephone Attorney General Robert Kennedy, the President's brother, to tell him that the killer was an ex-Marine who had defected to the Soviet Union and married a Russian. Hoover also said that the man was known to be a fanatical supporter of Fidel Castro, the Communist Prime Minister of Cuba. And by 4 p.m. the situation room of the White House communications center was informing newly sworn-in President Lyndon Baines Johnson that the assassination was the work of a loner and that no conspiracy to kill the President existed.

Then the story got even stranger. On the following Sunday morning, Oswald was being transferred between city and county jails when he was shot, in the basement car park of Dallas police headquarters. The killer was Jack Ruby, a small-time Dallas nightclub owner.

J.F. Kennedy		The World	
John ("Jack") Fitzgerald Kennedy is born in Brookline, Massachusetts.	1917		
		1918	World War I ends.
His father, Joe Kennedy, miraculously saves the family fortune by selling shares in advance of the Wall Street crash.	1929	1929	There is mass global unemployment as trade slumps in the Great Depression after the Wall Street crash.
Jack becomes a war hero commanding torpedo boats in the Pacific.	1943		
		1945	World War II ends.
Jack is elected to Congress.	1946		
		1949	China becomes a Communist republic.
		1950	War breaks out in Korea, with the U.S. supporting South Korea and China supporting Communist North Korea.
Jack Kennedy is elected to the Senate.	1952		
Kennedy marries socialite Jacqueline Lee Bouvier.	1953	1953	Soviet premier Stalin dies.
		1956	The Hungarian uprising is crushed by Soviet forces.
His book Profiles in Courage is awarded the Pulitzer Prize.	1957		
Kennedy is elected president.	1960	1960	Police in South Africa open fire on anti-apartheid demonstrators, killing 69.
The U.S. backs a coup in Cuba to remove Communist Prime Minister Castro; but the attempt fails.	Apr 1961	1961	The Berlin wall is erected by the East German government to stop its citizens escaping to the West. The human rights organization Amnesty International is founded, to campaign against the use of torture and for the release of political prisoners worldwide.
Kennedy orders a large increase in numbers of U.S. "military advisers" in South Vietnam.	Nov 1961		
Kennedy faces down Soviet premier Khrushchev's attempt to install nuclear missiles on Cuba.	1962	1962	Nazi war criminal Adolf Eichmann is hanged in Israel after Israeli agents abduct him from Argentina.
Kennedy initiates civil rights legislation in Congress.	May 1963	1963	Martin Luther King Jr. makes his "I have a dream" speech, calling for equality between whites and African Americans.
After Kennedy's efforts, the U.S., Britain, and the Soviet Union sign the Partial Nuclear Test Ban Treaty in Moscow.	Aug 1963		
Kennedy is assassinated in Dallas.	Nov 1963		
		1964	The U.S. Congress authorizes war against North Vietnam.
Jackie Kennedy marries Aristotle Onassis.	1968	1968	Martin Luther King Jr. is assassinated.

Above: The sixth floor of the Texas School Book Depository with the actual rifle the assassin used set up in the window. Below: The U.S. media was quick to agree with the view that Lee Harvey Oswald was the lone assassin.

Immediately after the assassination, President Johnson had set up the Warren Commission, under the chairmanship of Chief Justice Earl Warren, to find out what really happened. The F.B.I. conducted 25,000 interviews on the commission's behalf, and the Secret Service a further 1,550. The commission itself took testimony from 552 witnesses, of whom 94 appeared before it. Ten months later, it issued its 10-million word report. Its findings were stark and simple. Lee Harvey Oswald assassinated President Kennedy, acting alone. There was no conspiracy of any kind. Oswald was killed by Jack Ruby, who was also acting alone. Oswald and Ruby never met.

Oswald fired three bullets, it continued. The first missed. The second hit the President in the upper back and then struck Governor Connally, who was sitting immediately to the front of the President. The third and final shot killed the President by striking him in the right side of his head. According to the report, all the shots were fired within eight seconds or so from the Depository building, and no one else was involved.

It all seemed convincing—but was it the truth? Even before the Warren Commission reported, people were starting to ask questions and demand answers. Oswald was in no position to talk. Jack Ruby had seen to that. Ruby claimed that his motive for slaying Oswald was to spare Jackie Kennedy the emotional ordeal of testifying at a trial, but was that really believable? And too many of the commission's findings, said its critics, did not match—or chose to ignore—the facts.

What about the evidence from eyewitnesses who claimed to have heard shots coming from the area of a grassy knoll overlooking the plaza? If that was to be believed, there would have to have been at least two assassins—one on the knoll and one in the Depository. The commission simply dismissed even

Above: The President's limousine in Dealey Plaza just before the fatal shots were fired. Jackie Kennedy is seated next to her husband. Governor John Connally is immediately in front of the President.

Above: The limousine speeds away, heading for the emergency room of Parkland Hospital. You can just make out Secret Service agent Clinton Hill shielding the President and First Lady with his body.

the possibility that this could have been the case. What about the report's conclusion that the President and Governor Connally had been struck by the same bullet? According to the commission, the bullet passed through the President's upper chest and out of the front of his neck. It then struck Connally in the back, emerging from his right chest. It re-entered his body, breaking his forearm and coming out the other side of the wrist before ending up in his thigh—from where it fell onto a hospital stretcher, to be discovered virtually undamaged. How could one bullet do all that, especially since to do so meant that it somehow would have to have swerved in midair. It is scarcely surprising that the Warren Commission's critics promptly christened it "the magic bullet."

What about the precious seconds of film shot by Abraham Zapruder, a spectator in the Dallas crowd who provided the only visual record of the assassination? Frame-by-frame analysis seems to confirm that the shots had been fired too quickly to have all come from a single gun. Eventually, long after the Warren Commission had reported, fresh evidence was discovered—a police "dictabelt" that had recorded the sound of the actual gunshots. Acoustics experts said the recording proved that gunfire came not only from behind the President, that is from the vicinity of the Book Depository, but also from in front, that is from the grassy knoll. That meant that there must have been at least two gunmen. The recording also proved that there were four shots, not three, and that the third shot came from the grassy knoll.

Above all, what was Oswald's motive for killing the President? The Warren Commission skirted the issue by calling Oswald a "loner" and

PHOTOGRAPHS OF THE OSWALDS IN MINSK, U.S.S.R.

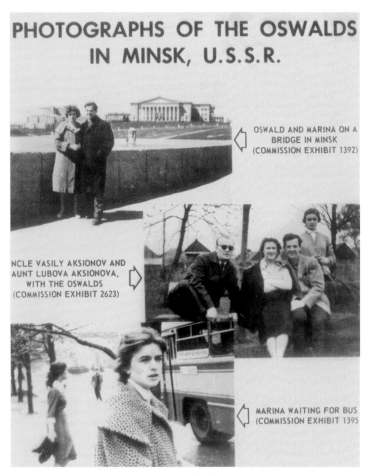

OSWALD AND MARINA ON A BRIDGE IN MINSK (COMMISSION EXHIBIT 1392)

NCLE VASILY AKSIONOV AND AUNT LUBOVA AKSIONOVA, WITH THE OSWALDS (COMMISSION EXHIBIT 2623)

MARINA WAITING FOR BUS (COMMISSION EXHIBIT 1395)

Above: Lee Harvey Oswald's decision to go to the U.S.S.R. in 1959 led to his undesirable discharge from the Marine Corps Reserve. Some think that his Russian wife, Marina, might have been a K.G.B. spy and the marriage was to get her into the U.S.

a "malcontent." It was true that Oswald had a murky left-wing past. He had immersed himself in Communist literature, lived for more than two years in the Soviet Union, and was heavily involved with Cuban revolutionary politics. But if the President's killing had been politically motivated and Oswald the left-wing fanatic that he was claimed to be, history shows that it is far more likely than not that the perpetrator would have claimed responsibility. Oswald did not. He fervently protested his innocence, claiming to be the victim of a frame-up. Indeed, the last words he shouted to reporters just before Jack Ruby killed him were "I am just a patsy!"

There are many other questions that the doubters say have never been satisfactorily answered. From the start, some of Oswald's co-workers at the Book Depository said that he was having lunch in the staff room on the first floor when the shots were fired. If he *had* fired the shots, would he have had the time to hide the rifle and run down from the sixth floor and out of the building to where Dallas police officers saw him once they arrived? Chemical tests on Oswald for gunpowder traces proved negative. And why, when it was relatively simple to buy a rifle and pistol over the counter, would a man intent on assassination buy them by mail order and have them sent to his own post office box? It is things like these that have led many to claim that the President's assassination must have been the result of a conspiracy.

Over the years, at least five major possible groupings of conspirators have been proposed. One theory is that the assassination was the work of a right-wing conspiracy within the U.S. government, involving the C.I.A. and J. Edgar Hoover, and that it was sparked off by President Kennedy's decision to withdraw U.S. military advisers from South Vietnam. Another is that it was down to right-wing dissidents outside the government, while a third blames anti-Castro Cubans and their supporters. The contrary belief is that the assassination was plotted by left-wing pro-Castro groups. The final theory is that the Mafia organized the killing in revenge for the President's decision to launch an all-out war against organized crime in America. But no conspiracy

"I am just a patsy!"

Lee Harvey Oswald, just before his murder by Jack Ruby, November 24, 1963

Above: Lee Harvey Oswald is interviewed during a break in his Dallas interrogation. He had been arrested in a movie theater watching the Audie Murphy movie War is Hell.

theorists have ever been able to produce hard evidence to back up their arguments and speculations.

Certainly, some odd events took place in Dallas before the killing. One theory is that, in the two months prior to the assassination, the conspirators, whoever they were, had an Oswald look-alike engage in various suspicious activities. He created a scene in a gun shop, fired shots on a woman's property and left behind a 6.5mm Mannlicher-Carcano cartridge case, hung around the Sports Drome Rifle Range, had his rifle repaired at a gunsmith's, and asked around about hotels with a good view of the downtown area. What we do know for sure is that the real Lee Harvey Oswald was elsewhere at the time these events took place. It seems someone was manufacturing evidence to make him look guilty.

Whatever the truth, the prosecution case against Oswald would have been far from watertight. His lawyers would have had plenty of material available to cast doubts in the minds of the jurors. Maybe, as one writer thinks, Oswald *was* involved but had "blundered into a quicksand of intelligence agents, Cuban exile plotters, and thugs, and the likelihood is that he was in over his head."

Had the idea of a "lone assassin" not bedeviled the investigation right at the start, police inquiries might have found the true killer (or killers). But as time passes, it becomes less and less likely that this mystery will ever be solved. The jury is still out on who was responsible and exactly what their motive was for gunning down President John F. Kennedy.

Below: Nightclub owner Jack Ruby slays Lee Harvey Oswald. The F.B.I. had been warned anonymously that Oswald would be shot during his prison transfer.

"All these incidents clearly cast suspicion on Oswald. Yet, the real Lee Harvey Oswald did not participate in any of them."

Michael L. Kurtz on the "look-alike" theory, Crime of the Century, 1982

FURTHER READING

1 Why Did the Pharaohs Build the Pyramids?

Herz-Fischler, Roger. *The Shape of the Great Pyramid*. Wilfrid Laurier University Press, 2000.

Jackson, Kevin, and Johnathan Stamp. *Pyramid: Beyond Imagination*. BBC, 2002.

Maisels, Charles. *Early Civilizations of the Old World*. Routledge, 1999.

Scarre, Chris, ed. *The Seventy Wonders of the Ancient World*. Thames and Hudson, 1999.

Siliotti, Alberto. *Guide to the Pyramids of Egypt*. White Star, 1997.

2 Who Built Stonehenge and Why?

Castleden, Rodney. *The Making of Stonehenge*. Routledge, 2002.

Champion, T., and others. *Prehistoric Europe*. Academic Press, 1984.

Darvill, T., and others. *England: An Archeological Guide*. Oxford University Press, 2002.

Gibson, Alex. *Stonehenge and Timber Circles*. Tempus, 1998.

Pitts, Mike. *Hengeworld*. Century, 2000.

Service, Alastair. *Lost Worlds*. Marshall Cavendish, 1981.

3 Was There a Trojan Horse?

Bahn, Paul, ed. *Lost Cities*. Weidenfeld and Nicholson, 1997.

Drews, Robert. *The Coming of the Greeks*. Princeton University Press, 1988.

Moorhead, Caroline. *The Lost Treasures of Troy*. Weidenfeld and Nicholson, 1994.

Wardle, K. and D. *The Mycenaean World*. Bristol Classical Press, 1997.

Wood, Michael. *In Search of the Trojan War*. BBC, 1998.

4 Did Rome Really Fall?

Connolly, Peter. *Greece and Rome at War*. Black Cat, 1988.

Howarth, Patrick. *Attila, King of the Huns*. Constable, 1994.

Reece, Richard. *The Later Roman Empire*. Tempus, 1999.

Rudgely, Richard. *Barbarians*. Channel 4 Books, 2002.

Swift, Ellen. *The End of the Western Roman Empire*. Tempus, 2000.

5 Was There a Real King Arthur?

Kirby, D. *The Earliest English Kings*. Unwin Hyman, 1991.

Ridyard, S., ed. *Chivalry, Knighthood and War in the Middle Ages*. University South Press, 1999.

Wood, Michael. *In Search of the Dark Ages*. BBC, 1991.

6 What Happened to the Knights Templars?

Partner, Peter. *The Knights Templar and their Myth*. Destiny Books, 1990.

Ralls, K. *The Templars and the Grail: Knights of the Quest*. Quest Books, 2003.

Read, Piers Paul. *The Templars*. Weidenfeld and Nicolson, 1999.

Robinson, J. *Dungeon, Fire and Sword: The Knights Templar in the Crusades*. M. Evans and Co., 1992.

Sora, Steven. *The Lost Treasure of the Knights Templar: Solving the Oak Island Mystery*. Destiny Books, 1999.

7 Was Marco Polo a Great Explorer or a Liar?

Larner, John. *Marco Polo and the Discovery of the World*. Yale University Press, 1999.

Polo, Marco. *The Travels of Marco Polo*. Modern Library edn., 2001.

Wood, Frances. *Did Marco Polo Go to China?* London, 1995.

8 Who Built Great Zimbabwe and Why?

Gazlake, Peter. *Great Zimbabwe*. Hazell, Watson and Viney, 1973.

Wilson, C. *The Atlas of Holy Places and Sacred Sites*. Dorling Kindersley, 1996.

9 Did the Chinese Beat Christopher Columbus to the New World?

Menzies, Gavin. *1421: The Year China Discovered the World*. Yale University Press, 1999.

Phillips, W.D. and C.R. *The Worlds of Christopher Columbus*. Cambridge University Press, 1992.

10 What is the Truth Behind the Legend of El Dorado?

Naipaul, V.S. *The Loss of El Dorado: A History*. Andre Deutsch, 1970.

Nicholl, Charles. *The Creature in the Map*. Jonathan Cape, 1995.

11 What Happened to North America's "Lost Colony?"

Durant, David N. *Raleigh's Lost Colony*. Atheneum, 1981.

Humber, John L. "Backgrounds and Preparations for the Roanoke Voyages, 1584–1590." *Raleigh*, Historical Publications, 1986.

Miller, Lee. *Roanoke: Solving the Mystery of the Lost Colony*. Arcade Publishing, 2001.

Quinn, David B. *The Lost Colonists: Their Fortune and Probable Fate*. N.C. Department of Cultural Resources, 1984.

Stick, David. *Roanoke Island: The Beginnings of English America*. University of North Carolina Press, 1983.

12 Why Did Japan Turn its Back on the World?

Keene, Donald. *The Japanese Discovery of Europe*. Stanford University, 1969.

Lehmann, Jean-Pierre. *The Roots of Modern Japan*. Macmillan, 1982.

Scott Morton, W. *Japan: Its History and Culture*. David and Charles, 1973.

13 Was King George III Really Insane?

Macalpine, Ida, and Hunter, Richard. *George III and the Mad-Business*. Pimlico, 1991.

14 Was Napoleon Poisoned?

Creston, D. *In Search of Two Characters*. Macmillan, 1947.

Weider, Ben. *Napoleon: The Man Who Shaped Europe*. Spellmount, 2000.

15 What is the Truth Behind the Myth of the Underground Railroad?

Blockson, Charles L. *The Underground Railroad*. Prentice-Hall Press, 1987.

Douglass, Frederick. *Life and Times of Frederick Douglass*. Collier Books, 1962.

Franklin, John Hope, and Schweninger, Loren. *Runaway Slaves: Rebels on the Plantation*. Oxford University Press, 2000.

McPherson, James M. *Battle Cry of Freedom*. Oxford University Press, 1988.

16 What is the Truth Behind Custer's "Last Stand?"

Connell, Evan. *Son of the Morning Star*. Pavilion, 1985.

17 Why Did the *Hindenburg* Explode?

Archbold, Rick. *Hindenburg: An Illustrated History*. Warner Books, 1994.

Bokow, Jacquelyn Cochran. "Fabric, Not Filling, to Blame: Hydrogen Exonerated in Hindenburg Disaster."

National Hydrogen Association News, Washington, D.C., 1997.

Dick, Harold G., and Robinson, Douglas H. *The Golden Age of the Great Passenger Airships: Graf Zeppelin and Hindenburg*. Smithsonian Institution Press, 1986.

Flynn, Mike. *The Great Airships: The Tragedies and Triumphs*. New York, 1999.

Horton, Edward. *The Age of the Airship*. Sidgwick and Jackson, 1973.

Toland, John. *The Great Airships: Their Triumps and Disasters*. Dover, 1999.

18 Was the Attack on Pearl Harbor Really a Surprise?

Gannon, Michael. *Pearl Harbor Betrayed: The True Story of a Man and a Nation under Attack*. Henry Holt, 2001.

Persico, Joseph E. *Roosevelt's Secret War: FDR and World War II Espionage*. Random House, 2001.

Prange, Gordon William. *At Dawn We Slept: The Untold Story of Pearl Harbor*. Viking Penguin, 2001.

Stinnet, Robert B. *Day of Deceit: The Truth About FDR and Pearl Harbor*. Free Press, 1999.

Toland, John. *Infamy: Pearl Harbor and its Aftermath*. Doubleday, 1982.

19 Did Lee Harvey Oswald Shoot President Kennedy?

Kurtz, Michael. *The Crime of the Century*. Harvester, 1982.

Scott, Peter. *Deep Politics and the Death of JFK*. University of California, 1993.

Scheim, David. *Contract on America*. Shapolsky, 1988.

INDEX

PICTURE CREDITS

Sources: ARPL = Ann Ronan Picture Library,
HIP = Heritage Image Partnership.

B = bottom, **C** = centre, **T** = top, **L** = left, **R** = right.

2/3 ARPL; **14T** HIP/British Museum; **14B** Edimedia;
15 Topfoto; 16 Edimedia; **17T** Edimedia; **17B** Topfoto;
18 Topham Picturepoint; 19 Corbis; 20 Edimedia;
21T Edimedia; **21B** HIP/British Museum; 22 Topfoto;
23 Edimedia; 24 HIP/British Library; 25 HIP/English
Heritage; **27T** Corbis; **27B** ARPL; 28 HIP/Public Records
Office; 29 Edimedia; 30 HIP/English Heritage; 31 HIP/
English Heritage; 32 Fortean Picture Library; 33 HIP/
British Museum; 34 Edimedia; 35 Edimedia; **37T** HIP/
British Library; **37B** Topfoto; **38TL** ARPL; **38BL** Edimedia;
38BR ARPL; 39 Edimedia; **40L** ARPL; **40R** Topfoto;
41 Topfoto; 42 ARPL; **43T** Edimedia; **43B** Edimedia;
45T Topfoto; **45B** Edimedia; 46 ARPL; **47T** Edimedia;
47B Edimedia; 48 Edimedia; 49 Edimedia; 50 Topfoto;
51T HIP/British Museum; **51B** Topfoto; 52 HIP/British
Library; 53 HIP/British Library; 54 Edimedia; **55T** Edimedia;
55B HIP/British Library; 56 HIP/English Heritage;
57T Topfoto; **57B** Topfoto; 58 Edimedia; **59L** Edimedia;
59R Edimedia; 60 ARPL; 61 Photos 12, Paris; **63T** Photos
12, Paris; **63C** Edimedia; **63B** Edimedia; 64 HIP/British
Library; 65 Photos 12, Paris; 66 Photos 12, Paris;
67 Photos 12, Paris; 68 Edimedia; **69L** HIP/British
Library; **69R** HIP/British Library; 73 The Bridgeman Art
Library; 74 The Bridgeman Art Library; **75L** Edimedia;
75R Edimedia; 76 Edimedia; 77 HIP/British Library;
78 Edimedia; 79 ARPL; 80 Edimedia; 81 Corbis;
83T Edimedia; **83B** Topfoto; 84 Corbis; 85 ARPL;
86 Edimedia; 87 Topham Picturepoint; 89 Corbis;
90T Topfoto; **90B** Topfoto; 91 Topfoto; **92T** Topfoto;
92B Topfoto; 93 Edimedia; 94 Edimedia; 95 HIP/Public
Records Office; **97T** HIP/British Museum; **97B** Edimedia;
98T HIP/British Library; **98B** ARPL; 99 ARPL;
100T Topfoto; **100B** Edimedia; 101 Edimedia; 102 HIP;
103 Corbis; **105T** Edimedia; **105B** HIP/British Library;

106 HIP/Public Records Office; 107 Corbis;
108 HIP/British Library; 109 ARPL; 110 Topfoto;
111T HIP/British Museum; **111B** Topfoto;
113T HIP/British Museum; **113B** HIP/British Museum;
114 HIP/British Library; 115 HIP/British Library;
116T HIP/British Museum; **116B** HIP/National Rail
Museum, York; 117 HIP/British Museum; **118T** Topfoto;
118B HIP/British Museum; 119 Topfoto; 120 Topfoto;
121L HIP/British Museum; **121R** HIP/British Museum;
122 Edimedia; 124 Edimedia; 125 HIP/Corporation of
London; 126 HIP/British Museum; 127 Edimedia;
128 Edimedia; 129 Edimedia; **131T** Edimedia;
131B Edimedia; 132 Photos 12, Paris; 138 Photos 12,
Paris; **133T** Photos 12, Paris; **133B** Photos 12, Paris;
134 Scala; 135 Edimedia; **136T** ARPL; **136B** Topfoto;
137 Edimedia; 138 Edimedia; 139 Edimedia;
141T Edimedia; **141B** Corbis; **142T** Topfoto;
142B Edimedia; 143 ARPL; 144 Edimedia; 146 Edimedia;
147B Edimedia; **147T** Edimedia; 148 Edimedia;
149 ARPL; 151 Topfoto; 152 Edimedia; 153 ARPL;
154 Edimedia; **155L** Edimedia; **155R** Edimedia;
157 Topfoto; 158 Edimedia; 159 Photos 12, Paris;
161T Corbis; **161B** Topfoto; 162 Corbis; 163 Corbis;
164 Topfoto; **165T** Corbis; **165B** Topfoto; 166 Topfoto;
167 Edimedia; 169 Topfoto; 170 Topfoto; 171 Topfoto;
172T Topfoto; **172B** Topfoto; 173 Topfoto; 174 Topfoto;
175 Topfoto; 176 Topfoto; 177 Gamma Presse;
178T Topfoto; **178B** Topfoto; **180T** Topfoto; **180B**
Topfoto; **181L** Topfoto; **181R** Topfoto; 182 Topfoto;
183L Topfoto; **183B** Topfoto.

Photo Research by Image Select International,
2a Marston House, Cromwell Business Park,
Chipping Norton, Oxfordshire OX7 5SR,
United Kingdom.

Grateful thanks are extended to Ann Asquith for her
valuable advice and assistance with the photo research
for this book.